BROTHER TOM

THE PEOPLE'S PREACHER

BY

ISBN: 978-0-9799919-0-5

Printed in the USA

CHAPTER ONE

GERMANY INVADES

I could not see in the dark, but I felt around the side of the alley until my left hand found a patch of dry grass. Then, I carefully put the hen's egg I had been cradling in my right hand in the center of the clump of grass and smoothed the tops of the limp grass over my treasure. Even if could not get my stolen egg tonight, perhaps I could find it tomorrow. Right now my mission was to find more food. Food for my growling eight-year-old stomach and food for my hungry parents and my four siblings.

Our situation in Werkendam must not have been much different from any other village or city in the entire country of Holland. Ever since the Germans had forcibly entered our country and occupied every town and city the year before, all of the Dutch citizens had to learn to adapt and cope to survive, or else.
And even at my young age, I knew what that else was. Sudden death, or deportation into concentration camps either in Holland, or worse yet, into the depths of Germany.

It was this fear that made me shiver as much as the cold night air that cloaked our town. My ears were sharply alert for the sound of heavy booted feet that meant some German patrol was out on the street with a bright flashlight that could spotlight anyone out in the dark after curfew.

I wiggled closer to the wooden fence and felt for the hole I had seen just that day. On the other side, I could smell the dried chicken droppings. I was close.

My exploring hands found the slight depression. It was not big enough for my slight body, but I dug the sandy soil away until I could squirm under the fence.

Every movement had to be made as softly as possible. Earlier night raids had taught me this. More than once I had to abandon my forays because some diligent watchdog heard my desperate attempts to hunt for food.

But lately, dogs were not as common. As difficult as it was for people to find food for themselves and their families, it was often too difficult to find food for dogs. So, dogs disappeared, perhaps sold as the meat of some other animal, and that made it slightly easier for me to enter the yards and scrounge for food.

But I knew the Sterkenburgs had hens. I had spied my hunting ground out the day before. There just might be several eggs in this hen house.

I wriggled out from under the fence and listened. There was no sound from the cottage at the far end of the yard. No light, either, but that was normal. No one was foolish enough anymore to let any light flicker out of the windows at night. Not since Widow Eens had been forgetful to cover her window with a blackout curtain and the patrolling German officer had fired through the window and killed her right in her home. That had been all the warning the rest of our town had needed.

I listened intently for a dog. I was not sure if Opa Sterkenburg still had his dog or not. The old man lived by himself and perhaps, he too, had gotten rid of his watchdog.

All was quiet. On careful, bare feet, I went across the hard packed dirt toward the hencoop.

I found the latch and swung open the hinged door. I heard a hen make an inquiring sound as hens do when they are not sure of what is happening. Slowly, I moved my right hand around inside the coop. My fingers were my eyes in the dark, and I mapped out the small area.

There! I felt the rough wooden side of a nesting box. I reached inside, and a tremor of joy surged through me when I discovered the two eggs nestled in the straw. Yes! We would have three eggs for breakfast the next day!

In my haste, I bumped against the tin water pan as I withdrew my hand clutching the precious eggs. The rattle upset the few hens and they began to cackle in alarm.

Not bothering to close the door, I dashed back to the fence and even as I flung myself to the ground, I heard a dog barking from inside the house.

Fear caused me to stuff the eggs in my pocket and I had barely begun my mad scramble to get under the fence when I heard the door open and Sterkenburg's voice. "Get him! Get the thief!"

Even though I was popping through the hole, I knew it would only take a few seconds for the dog to discover where I was. With shrill barks, he was coming toward me!

With a strangled cry, I pulled myself through the hole and jumped to my feet. I grabbed my wooden shoes and without pausing, raced away up the alley toward the dike.

Not until I was on the high road, running parallel with the canal did I stop to put my shoes on. Then, I began to stealthily go along the side of the road to muffle the sound of my klompen. The cobblestones always announced the passage of anyone foolish enough to walk on them with wooden shoes.

My heart was pumping rapidly from my near escape, but as the adrenaline rush diminished, I remembered my errand. Eggs!

Even before I plunged my hands into my pockets, I knew the answer. They were broken! I had been too scared to even think that of course, the eggs would be smashed in my wild scramble under the fence if they were unprotected as I had flung myself on the ground.

Despair surged through me even as I felt liquid seeping into my klompen. My precious eggs! Then, like a flash, I remembered the egg I had hidden in the grass. It would be too risky to go back and retrieve it. I only hoped it would still be there tomorrow.

"Cush, cush," I softly crooned as I stroked the side of the cow. I squatted beside the gentle creature and felt for her sagging udder. Carefully, I squirted milk into my tin pail. I made sure the stream of milk went against the side of the pail, for I could not afford raising another alarm by the distinctive, musical sound of the streams of milk on the bottom of a tin bucket. My earlier scare at Sterkenburg's yard had been enough for one night.

But it had been hunger that had made me venture out here to the edge of the town to where the Germans had allowed van Ellen to keep his two cows. There was precious little milk left over for the farmer after the officers had taken their quota, but even a little was better than nothing.

I knew there would even be less the next morning for the

hapless farmer, but my stomach did not really care about others right now. I was determined not to return empty handed that evening. Hunger was opening its ravenous mouth at my home. I was getting desperate.

This had not been the first time I had slipped into the pasture and taking a piece of rope, slipped it around the horns of one or the other of the placid cows, tied it to the fence and then taken a little milk from each of the quarters. Taking too much would have alerted the farmer and probably shut off the supply from me forever.

My little pail was not nearly full, but I stopped anyway. I untied the rope and freed the cow. Then, placing the cover on the pail, I quietly slipped through the wooden stake fence and replaced the stakes.

The first time I had entered the pasture, it had taken me quite a long time to work the bottom of four stakes loose and swing them sideways enough for me to slip through. But I had carefully pushed them back into place so nothing was noticeable through the day. So far, I had been fortunate.

It was late by the time I finally reached our fenced yard around the small cottage facing the alley leading to Hoogstraat. I left my klompen outside, still slithery inside from the broken eggs and slipped inside, barely opening the door wide enough for me to enter. My bare feet stuck to the floor as I walked through the back room.

"Tokie!" My mother used the nickname for Thomas. "It is late! Where were... are you all right?" She half whispered as she rose from her chair beside the dim candle.

The dark electric bulb dangled from the ceiling. There had been no electricity for months. The Germans had cut the wires leading to the village houses, unless they had requisitioned the houses for their own use.

"Are the little ones sleeping?" I asked, giving Mama the pail of milk. "Is Papa home?"

"Papa is not home," Mama whispered. "Yes, the little ones

are in bed. I am sure Reitze is not sleeping."

My older brother Reitze would probably be upstairs in our tiny bedroom, reading. A year older than I, he did not have the nerve to go scrounging for food. "Aren't you scared, Tokie, to go out in the night?" he would ask me, his dark eyes searching my face.

"Not me," I would laugh bravely, not admitting to anyone, not even to myself, the times when fear would turn my legs into jelly and my leaping heart wanting to jump out of my chest whenever I got into a frightening situation. "You know me," I would boast. "I love to get the best of the detested Germans!"

"Shh! Tokie!" Not only Reitze, but also my parents would caution me over and over again. "You are too brave, take too many risks!"

"But who brings home milk and eggs? Who gets food for us?" I would quiet their cautions with a shrug. "We eat when others starve."

Then no one would speak. These were desperate times, and desperate situations quelled many fears.

Mama had just poured a little of the precious milk into a tin cup and handed it to me when we heard the back door sigh as it was pushed open.

Two shadowy figures came into the room.

"Papa! Oom Peter!" My voice was barely a whisper, but even so, Papa placed his hand gently over my mouth.

Mama immediately blew out the candle and the room was plunged into darkness.

"Dear wife, do you have any food?" Papa asked softly.

"Tokie just brought in some milk," her voice came in a whisper. Then, we could hear the clinking sound as she removed the cover.

"Have the children had any?" Papa's voice trembled.

"Not yet. But you and Peter better drink it. You need it."

"Just a sip. Here, Peter."

With a sigh, Papa lowered himself onto a cot. "I am so tired. We have been walking since noon. All I want is some rest.

Tomorrow we can talk."

"Good night, Papa." I said as I headed for the narrow twisting stairs. "I am glad you are home."

"Tokie! Thank you for the milk. You are a brave lad." I could hear the emotion in my father's tired voice.

I scampered softly upstairs, tears stinging my eyelids. I could handle scary situations, but I did not know what to do with the tender feelings that came unbidden to my heart.

There was a flickering light beside the bed I shared with Reitze. Sure enough, he was still reading.

"Papa home?" he asked in a small voice.

"And Oom Peter," I answered. When I got in bed beside my brother, I sensed his apprehension. There always was an extra undercurrent of fear in the house whenever Papa showed up in the night. The fear of discovery.

After the first trainloads of German soldiers had arrived the summer before, all of us townspeople had watched in growing dismay as they conscripted the able young Dutch men and shipped them off to Germany for training, either as soldiers or as workers in the war factories.

When they began forcing the able-bodied men into conscription, whether they had families or not, my father and Oom Peter had slipped away into the darkness one night.

I still remembered that evening. Oom Peter had come after dark, and Papa and Mama had been talking about the recent developments.

"They are taking all the men up to age fifty," Oom Peter's voice was grim. "There will be no one left to take care of the women and children."

"It is true," Papa had agreed. "Only today I saw the notice for all the men to gather at the market square tomorrow for a meeting. That meeting will be the last we shall be seen in Werkendam."

"Oh! What shall we do?" I had heard the fear grip Mama's voice.

"The Biesbosch! We can hide in the Biesbosch!" Oom Peter's

voice urged.

Reitze and I had been in the darkened room, and I guess the grown ups had forgotten we were there. At first, I had not understood.

"Ahh!" Papa's voice seemed to grasp on that idea. "Just the place. We well know that swamp!"

The Biesbosch, or rush woods, was aptly named. The Waal and the Maas Rivers flowed into an inland arm of the sea, just downstream from our village. Silt, carried by the slow moving rivers, was deposited at the mouth by the tides that met the fresh water, caused a vast delta.

The Biesbosch was an important part of the local economy. It was there that the willows grew that formed the backbone of the cottager's livelihood. The trees were continually cut back to harvest the long willow branches that were used to make huge floating platforms. These willow platforms were weighted down by stones and formed the bottom of the dikes. Although the work was arduous, many of the men from our town worked there and were familiar with the treacherous places deep in the swamp.

Treacherous, because if some stranger did not know about the tides from the ocean, they could become marooned and stranded by the high tides.

"The Germans will not dare search the Biesbosch," Oom Peter said with conviction.

"Where will you sleep?" Mama's voice quavered.

"In the willow-owls' huts," Papa said. "There are many huts on the higher places where we can be out of the weather."

Willow-owls. That was the name given to the men who stayed for weeks, even months in the swamps. The huts were constructed of willow wands, simple, yet dry and secure.

"It is doubly important that you and I go," Oom Peter's voice held a note of urgency as he spoke to Papa. "If the Germans should find out that we are Jews..."

"Like Oom Joseph and his sister Tante Anneke De Fries?" The words burst out of my mouth.

I heard the sharp intake of my parents' breaths. "Boys! Are you still here?"

A chill settled over the house. We were Jews?

CHAPTER TWO

CHILD NO LONGER

"Tokie! Play the organ!" Mama was shaking me from beside my bed.

I sat up and sleepily rubbed my eyes. Oh, yes, Papa and Oom Peter were here. I scrambled for my clothes and followed Mama downstairs. The wooden floorboards were cold under my bare feet, but I was getting used to that. Hardly anyone in the entire family owned socks, and no one wore their shoes inside, much less the wooden klompen.

The old pump organ waited silently for me. I sat on the stool and limbered my fingers by flexing them above the keyboard. Then, I pressed with my bare foot on the right pedal, and began playing the first melody that came into my head.

As the pump organ began giving out its mellow tones, I heard footsteps overhead. I pumped harder, and played with gusto.

Then, I forgot about my surroundings as I gave myself over to the music. I had been playing the organ since I was five, sitting on Papa's lap as he guided my fingers over the keyboard while his feet pumped the organ for me. As soon as I could reach the pedals, I began playing by myself. I picked out any tune that I had heard, whether it was a patriotic melody or some simple folk tune. There were even times when I defiantly played the forbidden song, Wilhelmus, our national Dutch anthem. Mama would come rushing in and forbid me to play it.

"No, Tokie! You must not play that! If the Germans hear it, they will come and take you away!" I could hear the fear in her voice, and I would obediently go on to another tune.

But this morning, I knew why I had been drug out of bed early in the morning. Papa and Oom Peter were in the closet upstairs, listening to the radio. News from England, telling the Dutch what was really happening in the war that was holding our country, and many others, in the chilling grip of fear and uncertainty.

Playing the organ would drown out any words from the secret broadcasts. But I could not pause long between songs. Should some passerby hear the radio announcer and should it be reported to the Germans, we would be at risk of imprisonment.

We were only to know what the Germans wanted us to know.

"That kid must love his music," I heard a loud voice in German right outside the front of our house. "Anyone getting up so early to play some stupid Dutch folk song must be demented."

The words came clearly into the house. With a jerk, I began pumping furiously and the wheezy old organ responded to my fingers pounding on the keys. Anything, it did not matter what. I had to drown out the radio upstairs.

"O.K.," Mama tapped me on my shoulder, "you may stop playing."

"Mama, is there anything to eat?" My stomach was growling and my growing body cried out for food.

"I have some porridge left," Mama said wearily. "We must get something today. Perhaps Reitze can catch some fish from the river."

I hastily shoveled down the cold porridge Mama gave me. It was bland and tasteless, but at least it was food. Then, opening the back door, I slipped into my klompen and headed up the alley toward Hoogstraat. I knew where to go to find something.

I had not forgotten my hidden egg from the night before, but first of all, I had another stop to make. The de Vries Meat Shop. Today was butchering day!

My klompen echoed loudly on the cobblestone street as I ran through the market square. I entered Hoogstraat, where the shops faced each other and where already the store owners were opening up. True, there was hardly anything to sell, for our village had been almost cut off from the rest of the world since the occupation, but there were some merchants still in business.

"Heil Hitler!" I heard the German voices before I rounded a bend in the road to see a crowd gathered in front of the church. I pushed in among the townspeople to see what was happening.

The rowdy German soldiers had tied a rope around the steeple of the little church and anchored it to a large transport truck. A ring of soldiers, laughing and brandishing their guns, held back the crowd.

The motor of the truck roared and with a huge crash, the steeple toppled over onto the church house roof and then slid down onto the street, splintering into pieces.

I looked up at the soldier's face, standing right beside me. He eyes were bloodshot and he was cheering with the rest. His boisterous voice boomed out, "Heil Hitler! Er ischt unser gott!" (He is our god!)

For a moment, time stopped. At that moment, my nine-year-old consciousness registered that the world was truly a crazy place. That grown men would behave like hoodlums and destroy property just for anyhow, gripped me. Everything in that place was stamped on my mind clearly. The silent crowd of our people, watching with defeated eyes as a small group of foreigners destroyed their town, was devastating.

Why did no one do anything? Was there no one in that crowd with enough courage to rebel against this brainless action? Where was the pastor of the church? Did he not care that the soldiers were mocking his church?

Then I saw him, Pastor Leendert, standing with his shoulders bowed, looking at the ground. He stood by himself, and I saw many others in the crowd watching him. But the old man did not say anything, do anything.

For some reason, tears stung my eyelids. Tears of rage, frustration, and anger.

Then, I remembered where I had been headed and making a sharp right hand turn, I hurried toward the butcher shop.

"Tokie!" Annette de Vries greeted me cheerily when I raced through the front of the shop and entered the room where they cut up the meat. "Now, how about that! How is it that you knew to come today?" In spite of her age, her twinkling eyes in her merry, round face welcomed me as she took me by the arm and led me to the stove where a bit of delectable sausage was sitting at the edge of the pan, sizzling and giving out the most delectable smell. In a twinkling, she picked it up with a fork and then, slowly and tantalizingly, she moved it toward my mouth. I swallowed hastily as I salivated, and held my mouth open, my eyes closed.

"It was waiting just for you!" Tante Annette laughed cheerily as I rolled that delicious morsel around in my mouth.

"Go on," she laughed and spanked me lightly on my seat. "There are some lambs in the pen. Joseph will want to see you."

I went out the back door and hurried over to the holding pen. "Ahh! Tokie! I wonder what brings you here so early? It has nothing to do with what day it is, does it? Have you visited Annette?" Joseph, Annette's brother, called to me from the wooden loading dock.

"The visit to Tante Annette tasted good!" We laughed together.

I pushed away the dark cloud that had fallen on me from the scene by the church. The yells of the German soldiers seemed far away here in this cheerful spot with Joseph and Annette de Vries. There was always something exciting happening here. I rubbed the wooly little lambs and tried not to think of what would happen to them in another week. I wanted to think of happy things. Death was too common.

"Help me put the lambs into this pen and then I have to go upstairs and change into clean clothes. Can you imagine what the customers would say if they saw me with these clothes, cutting up meat?" Joseph lowered his voice and his eyes grew wide in mock alarm.

"Or Tante Annette," I chuckled as I looked at his barnyard overall that was dirty and stained.

I knew that their business was almost nonexistent, except for the Germans who demanded a steady supply of meat and seemed to never bother to pay for their "purchases". The de Vries' lived upstairs above their market and I could see in their lined faces that poverty was not resting lightly on their lives. Two years into the occupation, the strain was beginning to tell on everyone.

I had just left the shop and turned toward the market square, when I heard the noisy roar of a German army truck head towards me. I backed against the front of a house and turned to see where it was headed.

To my dismay, I saw the truck stop in front of the de Vries meat shop and a group of eight German soldiers jumped out and kicking open the front door, they filed inside.

Immediately, a crowd of townspeople gathered in the street to watch what was happening. I pressed as close as I could.

I heard a muffled scream from inside the shop, and then to my horror, I saw Tante Annette pushed ruthlessly out the front door, and almost falling from the shove.

"Get in!" The two soldiers that followed her yelled at her, propelling her toward the back of the truck.

Tante Annette tried to pull herself up, but she seemed too scared to have enough strength to get up into the back of the truck. "Get in!" one of the soldiers yelled and struck her with his club.

The scream of fear and pain from the old woman split the air of the street. She scrambled wildly just as her brother came flying out the door, stumbling and falling on his face in the street.

I thought I could not bear to watch, but something held my eyes to the scene in front of me. I could not look away.

The soldiers blocked my view of Oom Joseph, but I could see their clubs rise and fall on the hapless victim. "Filthy Jew! Pig! Scum of the earth!" The German words spewed out the soldier's mouths until they had heaved the beaten man into the back of the truck. Six of the soldiers jumped in with them and with a roar, the truck left us with a stench of diesel smoke.

My hands were clenched tightly, and I ground my teeth in rage. Hot, angry tears again scorched their way down my cheeks as I turned and fled.

"But they gave me sausage! They were so kind to me!" My words made no sense, even to me, but Mama seemed to understand. I had burst into the house, scaring my three little sisters.

"Mama! Mama! They have taken Tante Annette and Oom Joseph! The Germans took them and I know they will be killed!" My words came out, hot and jerky.

Mama had immediately put her hand over my mouth and told Jurriana, "Take the little ones outside in the back yard."

"They are Jews," Mama had tried to explain. "The Germans found out they are Jews. Hitler is trying to rid the entire world of all the Jews."

"But, we...we..."

Again Mama put her hand over my mouth and shook her head warningly. "Tokie, no! Never mention it anywhere! Do you understand?" Her eyes glittered strangely and she seemed possessed with another spirit. She leaned closely to me and said in a whisper, her breath sending a coldness into my ear. "No one knows! We have been here in Werkendam for many years and no one knows! It must stay that way."

I said no more. Then, I stood up and with my eyes only, motioned upstairs.

"Gone," Mama said briefly. I knew Papa and Oom Peter had somehow slipped out. Perhaps they had heard the commotion that morning by the church and used that opportunity to leave.

I remembered my egg hidden in the grass. I went outside and retraced my steps from the night before. My scalp prickled when I saw the board fence where I had wriggled under the night before and I of course noticed the hole carefully filled up again. Nevertheless, I knelt down and hunted among the dry grass clumps for my hidden egg.

Nothing. I searched for a long time and did not find my egg. A dull sense of hopelessness filled me. I wanted to strike out at something. I kicked against a wooden post with my right foot and even protected by my wooden klompen, I felt a sharp pain race up my leg.

I limped away, not caring where I went. All I could see was that horrifying image of the de Vries being beaten and carried off. Something inside of me seemed to shrivel up and die. I think right there I left my childhood and was forced into a cruel and unjust world.

From then on, I intensified my hunt for food and courted

danger with a reckless abandon. Something inside of me hardened and I was willing to take bold and daring risks. I laughed at death and danger.

"Tokie! Get up!" I felt a strong hand shake me. Papa!

"They got him! They caught Oom Peter!" The ragged panting of Papa's voice brought me wide awake.

He was breathing hard. "The German soldiers caught him just outside of town, going toward the Biesbosch. Quick, get dressed and see which way they are taking him! Watch to see if they go toward Sleeuwijk or if they head toward Nieuwendijk at the fork in the road. They are on foot!"

Before Papa had finished speaking, I had dressed and was on the way down the stairs. Papa followed.

"They caught us by surprise. Oom Peter was going first and I was following.

"The soldiers were beside the road, down the bank. When they heard Peter, they came up and grabbed him. I rolled over the bank on the other side and they did not know there were two of us." I was out the door and running barefooted down the alley. Fear, blended with excitement, lent speed to my legs and I ran as fast as I could.

I was outside town when I saw the group of men ahead. Oom Peter was not the only prisoner. I could see four other men walking in single file behind my uncle. They had their hands clasped behind their heads and were guarded by a soldier in the front, and one in the back. The soldiers both carried guns.

I would follow them. I stayed behind, pretending to be merely curious.

The tall, burly German guard in the rear glanced back and saw me. "Get away! Schnell!" he yelled brandishing his gun.

I guess I thought for some reason he would not shoot at me. I was only a boy, following along to see what was happening. So, I did not leave, but fell behind only slightly.

"Eyes ahead!" That command was for the prisoners. Must

be someone had dared to try to look back to see who was following.

I followed closer. The big German saw me and said with a roar. "Now you get out of here, you little Dutch boy! Go home!"

His tone of voice should have scared me more than it did, but even so, I only fell back a few yards more. I was determined to find out where they were taking their prisoners.

We had only gone a little further, when the rear guard turned around again. When he saw me, he yelled, "I'll kill you, you little pig!" and before I could react, he fired at me.

Instantly, I fell to the ground, crashing onto the dirt road and rolling over onto the grass.

It all happened so fast, I had no time to think. Yet, there was an automatic reaction inside me to pretend I had been killed.

I heard cries from the prisoners and distracted yells from the two guards. "Line up! No looking back! I'll shoot!" The German words came fast and furious.

When the furor had died down, I heard approaching footsteps. Booted steps. Soldier steps.

I lay perfectly still, my left arm twisted up over my face, my head hanging downhill, almost in the drainage ditch.

I felt a boot nudge my leg. I did not move.

"Leave the little pig and come back here!" The other guard was clearly nervous, watching his five prisoners carefully.

"He's dead already," I heard the voice above me say and then I heard him walking away.

I lay beside the road a long time after I could no longer hear anything from the group of marching men. In spite of my bravado, I realized how close to death I had been.

I still don't know what saved me from the German's bullet. Did he miss because he had to swing his gun around to fire, or did I drop instinctively when I saw him aim at me? All I know is, I did not die that day.

Finally, I dared raise my head and crawl back up beside the road. I could see far down the flat landscape and just in time, I saw them turn toward the neighboring village of Sleeuwijik. I waited until they vanished around the bend, then I raced back home.

"They took them toward Sleeuwijik!" I gasped when I was back upstairs. Papa nodded and disappeared downstairs and I heard him leave through the back door.

I lay exhausted on the bed and wondered about the fate of Oom Peter. Would they send him off to Germany? Would they discover he was a Jew and send him to his death in some concentration camp? Rumors were rampant about the hundreds of Jews exterminated in death camps.

"He is safe," Papa came home late that night and woke up Mama and Reitze and I. "The Dutch Resistance movement surprised them, bound up the Germans and left them beside the road, took their uniforms and rifles, and freed all the prisoners."

"Where is Oom Peter?" I asked.

"Biesbosch," Papa replied. "Where I am going. For a long time."

When Papa had gone outside, ready to join Oom Peter, I followed him. "Did they kill the German soldiers?"

"Tokie, it is enough for you to know that the prisoners are safe. You did your part well and do not ask questions. It is better that you do not know these things. You are too young."

I had my answer. I was sure someone from the resistance movement had killed those soldiers. I was glad. I hated all the Germans.

I crept upstairs. I had told no one about my near death. I would keep it to myself.

"Are you scared?" Reitze asked as we lay in bed, side by side. "You are shaking."

I did not answer. All was dark around me.

My anger was not only against the Germans. There were some weaklings in our village that cottoned to the Germans, trying to win their favor by alleging they were loyal to Hitler and his regime. These people were given pseudo jobs and positions that held no real power. I saw more than once that if the German soldiers were in bad moods, these traitors received the same treatment as anyone else. But, I despised the Dutch who fell into the German trap and tried to rule over their fellow townspeople with their new "responsibilities".

I got even in the only way I knew.

There were times when the Germans brought food in for the villagers by truck. The food was of very poor quality, but yet I guess they knew if they would starve all of us, there would be an uprising, so they pretended to care for us by bringing in food.

Jan Arie liked his important job of alerting the people whenever the food was available. He would yell at the people lining up for their portion and smile benignly at us as the Germans watched.

One day, I had enough. I hatched up a plan.

I got up early in the morning, just at crack of summer dawn. I went to the edge of the village with a pail and gathered my ammunition from the manure pile.

The day before, I had helped the farmer gather all the eggs that were still in the nests of the hatchery that had not hatched. We had carefully put them in a pail, because we did not want the risk of breaking those rotten and extremely smelly eggs.

"Put them in the manure pile, but do not break them!" the farmer had warned me. "My wife will not let me in the house if the stench of rotten eggs clings to my clothes."

Since their farm was right on the edge of the village, he also did not want to raise the ire of the neighbors by exposing them to the heady, ripe smell of rotten eggs.

It was then that I had hatched my plan.

So now, early in the morning, I carefully gathered a pail full of the rotten eggs and went back to Hoogstraat.

In good Dutch fashion, all the people of the town left their klompen outside their doors. I quietly slipped an egg in each klompen until my pail was empty.

Then I sneaked over to where Jan Arie always stood to strike the brass gong.

I reached up and struck the gong hard, three times.

Before the last echo died out, I was gone, running like the wind back home. I did not pause, but raced upstairs and slipped under the covers beside my sleeping brother. I drew in slow breaths to ease my heavy breathing and even closed my eyes.

It must have been barely ten minutes later when I heard a commotion outside.

"Bring that young boy outside! He must be at the bottom of this!" I heard Jan Arie's loud booming voice bellowing in our alley.

I heard my mother open the door. "What is the matter?" Her voice was sharp and shrill, like a good Dutch housewife's should be.

"Where is your son? That Thomas?"

"Upstairs sleeping. Like I would be if you would not have come and woke up our entire household. Eew! Why do you stink like rotten eggs? What do you want?"

Jan Arie must have quailed just a little under the onslaught from my mother's voice. And tone. "He...Someone put rotten eggs in the klompen and then rung the brass gong! The people on Hoogstraat are furious and the smell is everywhere!" At the thought of the indignity, he became belligerent. "I will report this to the German officer! He will look into this matter. Where is Thomas?"

"I will get him," Mama said firmly. "You stay out there. I do not want your smelly feet in my house."

"Reitze! Tokie! Get up!" Mama called up the stairs.

Reitze sat up in bed. I continued to "sleep".

"What is it, Mama?" Reitze asked.

"Get up! Is Tokie there?"

"Yes. He is sleeping," Reitze replied.

There was silence and then I heard her from the back door. "My sons are both upstairs, sleeping."

"Get that Thomas out here," Jan Arie demanded. "I want to see him!"

"What have you done?" Reitze grabbed my shoulder and shook me. "Jan Arie is mad!"

I sat up in bed and tried to look bewilderingly at my brother. "Why?"

"Get up! Come down right away," I heard the stern note in my mother's voice and we both went downstairs.

"Here are both my boys," Mama shoved us out the back door. "Are you satisfied now?" She glared at Jan Arie and then drew us back inside. "You may leave now and take your "fragrance" with you." She shut the door firmly.

I thought I was going to get more satisfaction from my stunt than I really did. People avoided Hoogstraat for several days and mistrusted Jan Arie even more than before. In spite of his protestations, there were still people that felt he had done this to humiliate them, in spite of the fact that his own klompen had been "egged".

Rumors were that the Germans had thought the entire episode a hilarious incident and laughed at Jan Aries when he had reported it to them.

Even then, I was glad that Jan Aries had no friends. The townspeople had their own clever ways of shunning him and even the Germans had not been sympathetic to his plight. I thought he deserved it all.

CHAPTER THREE

HANS & WALTER

I burst in the front door of our small house. "Where's Reitze?" I asked Mama.

"He took the little girls on a walk," Mama said. Then, in an undertone, she added, "There are two of them upstairs."

I felt my blood boil. I clenched my fists and stared at the ceiling of our downstairs room.

"Now, Tokie, don't start anything," Mama warned firmly, yet quietly.

That was the way life was during the occupation. For no apparent reason, our homes where entered and searched at random by the soldiers. Without asking permission, the front door was kicked open and the house could suddenly be filled with uniformed men, checking out the premises.

Would they find the radio this time, I wondered? I did not know where Papa hid our link to the free world, but every time our house was searched, we all wondered if the radio would be discovered.

"They have been up there a long time," Mama said, rubbing her hands together. I knew she was nervous. She walked across to the front window and looked out. Then, she pulled the lace curtains together again at the center.

"See if you can sneak upstairs and see what is going on," Mama told me. "I think they are in your room."

I went softly up our narrow, twisty stairs, carefully stepping on the edge of each worn board. I knew which treads squeaked and avoided them by skipping the squeaky ones.

There were only two rooms in our upstairs, and both entrances were off the square landing in the middle of the house. Usually, the doors stood open, but this time, the door to my room was closed. I heard a muffled sound coming from inside. I cocked my head, but could not identify the sound. It didn't sound like any German soldier's voice I had ever heard. The tone was soft, almost as if choked by tears!

I eased forward and bent over to look through the keyhole.

I had a sideways view of the scene in my bedroom, the little window at the gable end illuminating something I had never imagined in my short span of years. Those German soldiers were kneeling side by side, their heads bowed, and even though their voices were muffled, I could hear them praying! Not only praying, they were wiping their streaming eyes. They were crying, too!

I retreated downstairs and when Mama saw me, she said urgently, "Tokie, what is it?"

My words sounded strange to my own ears. "They are praying! They were crying!" I took a deep breath and when I realized my mouth was hanging open, I licked my dry lips and closed my mouth.

Mama leaned forward and peered at me. "No! German soldiers don't pray. They kill and steal and destroy, but they don't pray!"

All I could do is nod my head dumbly.

Our family was not religious. Like I said earlier, I did not even know we were Jews until Reitze and I had overhead that earlier conversation between my parents and Oom Peter.

Yet, I knew what prayer was. I had had a brush with religion even before the war.

Werkendam was known as a very religious town. Five churches graced our village, each one a different denomination. Most of the townspeople attended their church faithfully and determined that the town would be kept under the strict rule of the religious officials. That was before the war, of course.

I remember vividly one Sunday, I must have been barely six, when I was outside, riding my bicycle. Suddenly, I was seized by the ear and a black-coated man led me to the front door of our house, never letting go of my aching ear.

"If you want to do business in this town, you make sure that your family observes the rules of the Sabbath." He pushed me into the house and my bicycle fell onto the cobbles.

Yes, I knew about prayer. I had heard the congregations through the open windows on Sundays as I went about my errands. I even knew that since the occupation, even more people attended church than in peacetime. I sensed that somehow they were searching for something.

There was even a brief time that I had been inveigled by some of my friends from school to join them in their catechism class. Back then, I did not think much made sense that the teacher taught us, but there were odd times afterwards that suddenly, out of the blue, something would come to me that I knew I had heard from that class.

I had been rather forcibly ejected from the class one day when two of my friends and I had "discovered" the communion wine and decided if the adults drank it twice a year, it must be good.

In spite of the unexpected flavor, I remember it sent a warm feeling over my food-hungry body, and we kept on drinking until the bottle was empty.

Then, we had entered the class where the teacher had already begun the lesson for that day.

We stumbled rather than walked to our seats, singing something that was definitely not fitting for a church class and things after that deteriorated rather swiftly. No one seemed to appreciate our witty answers to the questions that were asked.

My parents did the usual parent thing. I was whipped and sent upstairs to bed to sleep off my stupor. After that, they forbade me to return to the catechism class.

So, that was my basic brush with religion. Now, to have looked through the keyhole onto that scene in my bedroom was a total shock.

"Are you sure they are praying?" Mama's voice shook me out of my reverie. "They are awfully quiet."

"I'll look again," my curiosity led me back up the stairs. As I bent over to peer through the keyhole again, the door opened and a big, meaty hand grabbed my shirt front. In my curiosity, I must have forgotten to step over the creaky tread and alerted them to my spying.

I looked up the row of buttons on the soldier's uniforms until my eyes looked straight into his face.

We stood there silently, looking at each other. The other

soldier joined us in the doorway.

My legs began to buckle in spite of my firm resolve not to show fear. I imagine they saw my white face, for the one in the back said, "Walter, let him go. He is scared."

The hand released me. "Don't be afraid, sonny," the voice was actually kind. "We need you to do something for us."

Was I asked to be a collaborator? One of the despised townspeople who turned traitor and aided the Germans? "First, you must promise never to tell anyone what you saw." Walter said in as stern a voice as he could manage. "We will kill you...." he broke off and said over his shoulder.

"Hans, there I go again. You see what this war has done to us? Made us into killing machines! Either killing or threatening to kill! God, forgive me!"

My mind was in a whirl. Whatever was going on here? At first, they were praying soldiers, then they turned into typical soldiers, and now, this? It didn't make sense.

I saw tears brimming in Walter's eyes. "Look, sonny, let me try again.

"We need two sets of your daddy's clothes. We need them," he reiterated softly. "But it would be better if no one ever knew about this. Not even your mama. It would be better if we should ever be discovered.

"You look like a bright young lad. We are putting a lot of trust in you by asking this favor.

"For the rest of the day, we will be up here. This is your room, right?"

I nodded. "My brother and I sleep here."

"If sometime today, you can get us two sets of your father's clothes, you will be doing your country and your village a great favor. But I cannot tell you how important it is for you to remain absolutely quiet about this. Do you understand?" Walter looked down at me, his eyes searching my face.

Something about their sincerity, their desperate eyes, made me nod my head.

"Shake," Hans stuck out his right hand.

I reached up and shook his hand, and then Walter offered me his hand.

For a moment, I forgot they were German soldiers. I forgot that they represented the hated repressive regime that had swept into our lives and changed everything.

Walter's strong hand was warm as it closed around my fingers. He smiled at me.

"What are they doing?" Mama asked me sharply. "I heard them talking to you. Did they discover...?"

"No," I whispered. "They didn't."

With furrows creasing her forehead, Mama asked again. "What are they doing?"

"They said they are going to stay in my room for the rest of the day." I did not really know what else to say.

"Oh, no," Mama groaned. "They will make me nervous, being overhead the rest of the day. What if...."

I shrugged my shoulders. I could not explain what was going on inside of my mind.

Those Germans had ceased to be the enemy. They were just two ordinary men now, not even soldiers. They had feelings, emotions, and I could tell they had many questions of their own.

"I am going out, Tokie! I will not stay in this house with them upstairs! It will drive me crazy!" Mama got to her feet and grabbed her jacket.

"You stay here, Tokie, and watch what they do! You are never scared and you can..." She stopped her chatter and looked at me. "Oh, I don't know what you can do, but you can do it better than I could."

I knew she was thinking about my night time forays into the dark to steal eggs, milk, or whatever I could find for us to eat. Over and over my family would tell me that I was the one that was never scared.

"I'll stay," I said bravely. This was really one time when I was not scared at all. Not scared, but I was bewildered. Bewildered by my own feelings.

After dark that evening, two men slipped from our house, dressed in my father's clothes. They left from the upstairs window, down across the back room roof and through our back yard.

"Now that's a strange way for soldiers to disappear," Mama laughed nervously when I told her that they had left. "Are you sure they are gone?"

We were gathered around the table, eating our skimpy supper.

"Yes, they are gone," I assured her. "I saw them climb out the window."

Mama heaved a sigh of relief.

It was only a few days later that Papa came home for the night. That evening, I played the organ again with vigor, singing at the top of my voice. I knew that Papa wanted to hear the latest news on the radio. I played for over an hour, and then only stopped because our neighbor Leny yelled at me. "Stop, now, Tokie! I can't sleep!"

Mama, App and I crowded into our parents' bedroom to hear the update. "The Allies continue to tell us to be patient," he said in a weary voice. "For over two years now, that is what we are told. Help is on the way, but we need to be patient." His voice was bitter.

"I know some are not willing to wait. There are places where we can still strike the enemy where it hurts!" Papa stared into the dark, deep lines reaching out from his eyes.

"But something strange happened," he turned and looked at Mama. "We got news that two German soldiers, dressed in civilian suits, were trying to defect from the army.

"They must have decided to hide out in the Biesbosch, but they did not know enough about our swamp and they were discovered by the Germans. They were both shot." He paused for a moment, and then shrugged his shoulders. "They were Germans, so who cares what they were after."

He continued to talk, but I heard no more. I left their room and crawled into bed. I pulled the covers up over my head. I did not want to think.

But visions of Hans and Walter, kneeling right beside this bed, came unbidden into my mind. I was acutely aware of the mattress beneath me and that here, something had happened to those two men. I had seen sorrow, regret, and remorse written across the faces of those two German men. I had been moved by something in their lives that day that I did not have words for.

Now they were dead.

Or were they? Did the God they prayed to hear them? Was there Someone Who really did look out for and hear the desperate cries of hurting hearts? I did not know, and tossed for hours, sleepless.

But most of my sympathy left for any German only a few days later.

My younger sister Jurrie and I were out in the countryside, begging food from farmers when right on the road in front of us, it was as though gigantic hail fell from the sky and made mini-craters all over the blacktop. The scream of jet fighters overhead and mortar shells pounding the earth turned our serene Dutch countryside into a battlefield as airplanes roared over head in combat.

To this day, I have no idea how we survived. I remember hugging my screaming sister to my chest and cowering on the bank of the dike, trying to press ourselves into the dirt as the battle raged around and over us. For several long, dreadful minutes it lasted, and then the engines roared away into the distance.

I don't know how long we lay there, shivering with fright in spite of the warm summer air. When we finally crept up the bank and looked around, it was as though the world had ended.

All around lay charred and burning debris from wreckage. The road looked as though a gigantic tractor had plowed it.

Jurrie was still shaking with sobs as we worked ourselves

around the rubble and headed back to town.

"We flew!" Jurrie said in wonderment as we got closer to home. "We flew through the air!"

I nodded my head. I knew something extraordinary had happened. Reality told me we should have been dead, lying beside the road we had been walking along. There was nothing that made any sense to what had happened.

How could we have been carried through the air, both of us, down the dike to the edge of the canal by any force and not even been injured? Any explosion should have killed us, rather than just have thrown us through the air and landed us gently in a depression on the bank.

The more I thought about it, the less explanation I had. I looked up into the blue sky.

Was there a God up there? Did He look after children? Had He sent some angel, some mighty power, and carried us to a place of safety as soon as the dogfight in the sky had started?

But by the time we had reached home, my old familiar feeling of bitterness and anger at the Germans had pushed away our miraculous rescue.

It was all the Germans' fault. This whole mess; my father and uncle in hiding, the de Vries' brutal removal from their meat market, Hans and Walter trying to defect and being killed by their own countrymen, and our constant struggle to stay alive in this war-torn village. Hate boiled up inside me.

CHAPTER FOUR

SAVED FOR A REASON

I had just gone out the back door into the snow covered back yard, when I heard an army truck come roaring up the street and stop right by our front door.

"They found out Papa is hiding upstairs!" My first wild thought made me dash inside.

"Mama!" I yelled in a hoarse whisper. Reitze was wide-eyed by the front window.

"Boys, sit down and feed your sisters," Mama said sharply. "This is just a normal day." But I could tell she was scared, because the hand that smoothed her hair was shaking.

"Open up!" The commanding voice yelled outside.

Mama unlocked the door.

Two soldiers entered our house. They did not wave their guns around or even look threatening.

"There he is," one of them said, looking straight at me. "That's the one!"

A whole list of incidents flashed through my mind. What had they found out?

The other one laughed. Then, he looked at our scared faces. He walked over to my mother and bent over, speaking right into her face. "We want that young boy of yours to come and play for our Weinachtsdag, our Christmas! We have heard him play the organ in your house when we pass by and we need him to come help us celebrate!"

They were already slightly drunk. I could tell.

The first one reached out and tugged at my arm. "Come, sonny. What is your name? Tokie? O.K. We will take good care of you if you come play for us." Then turning to Mama, he swept his cap off and bowed tipsily. "Thank you for the Christmas present of your son. But of course, you will get this present back again!"

Mama shoved my pitiful coat at me as I trotted between the two soldiers out to their truck.

"Hey, is that the musician? Good, good, you got him!"

I had never before had a ride in a German army truck. My adventurous spirit soon rose and I actually enjoyed the ride to the officers' barracks.

There, for three days, I was plied with food and drink and seated at the organ to play for the merry makers. The walls rang with laughter and the partying lasted day after day. I played every song I could remember, and when the soldiers knew the melody, they sang along. Late at night, if I grew tired, I would stumble to some sofa and collapse, sleeping in my clothes.

It was on the fourth day, late in the evening, that I gathered as many cakes and cookies as I could and escaped into the night. By that time, I think they were getting tired of partying and no one stopped my exit. The guards shrugged their shoulders when they saw me leave and resumed stomping their feet to keep warm in the frigid air.

"Where ever have you been, Tokie?" Mama's voice was sharp with relief when I finally stumbled into our house.

"Look!" I showed her the cakes and cookies I had been carrying. "It is Christmas!"

"For them, but not for us!" Mama said sharply, and then took a bite out of a cookie. I knew that she was as hungry for decent food as anyone.

"We will save the rest for tomorrow," I heard her voice fade away as I flopped down on the sofa. I was bone tired from my three day hiatus.

"Hsss!" I heard the alert as soon as I entered our back yard after dark. Instantly, I stopped.

"Who is there?" I said in a low voice.

"Papa," came the reply from the garden shed.

I tensed. It had been several months since Papa had come home from his hiding place in the Biesbosch.

"I need your help," Papa whispered. "Come with me. I am going across the Nieuwe Merwede to see how Oom Jacob and Tante Janneke are faring. No one has heard from them for months."

"I'll come," I replied. At twelve, I was ready for any adventure during our occupation. The four years had dragged along, each successive year becoming more and more difficult for us the find food, much less clothes. My mama had resorted to sewing me a suit out of an itchy wool blanket, the color of green mud. I was wearing that suit now, and although I know I looked like something that crawled up out of the swamp and I was red from constantly scratching where it itched against my bare body, it did do two things. It warmed me and kept me dry. During this last winter on my forays for food, those two things had become increasingly important.

"How do we get across the river? It is being watched." I was curious to know Papa's plan.

"Just come," Papa said and I followed him.

A boat! I had not know Papa had been able to get a boat. He must have bought it on the black market, for the Germans did not allow any of the townspeople to own boats. They were considered too dangerous, lest the resistance movement mobilized against them.

"Here, hold this. Don't let it get wet!" Papa handed me a bundle wrapped in paper and tied with string. "Food for Jacob and his family," he explained tersely.

I lifted the parcel and sniffed. Meat! There was dried beef in there! And I could feel a loaf of bread.

The wooden boat was small and I sat in the prow while Papa began to row. The water was choppy for a wind was sweeping across the surface. In the distance, I could see a searchlight piercing the darkness, turning in timed circles, beaming out over the broad river.

Papa rowed steadily, bringing us ever nearer the powerful light.

"When the light comes," Papa told me, "duck down low into the boat so it will not pick up our forms."

I watched the sweep of light come across the water. I ducked down inside the low-riding boat. Papa did the same.

The light swept over us. Immediately, Papa began to row again.

The next time, I called out, "Light!" before it reached us, so Papa could duck. His back was toward the circling beam and it made it easier for him to know just when to lay low.

On and on into the night we rowed. We, because I took my turn and let Papa rest. I enjoyed the exercise, and it warmed me up. The wind was chilly and the night air damp. Even though it was late March, our country does not warm up much until at least the last of April.

When we finally reached the shore, we pulled the boat up into the rushes, took the parcel, and I followed Papa up the bank over the dike and down into a small polder.

Dawn was already streaking the east and I realized how far we had traveled. My sleepy brain told me we had been on the water all night.

The simple wooden cottage sat sheltered under several trees. I had dim memories of having visited my relatives when I had been younger.

"Hello!" Papa knocked on the door and called out, "It is Gerrit Visser!"

There was no reply.

Papa pushed the door open and an odor came out of that dank house that still haunts me today.

In a flash, Papa was inside. I peered in through the open door and covered my nose with my hand.

My uncle lay motionless on the sofa. I knew he was dead.

But my father was kneeling beside the bed where Tante Annette lay.

"Gerritt," my aunt looked up at his face. "You have come!" Then, in a weak voice she murmured, " Willemina!"

I looked in the corner and saw my eight year old cousin, huddled under a blanket. She was propped up on a bed of clothes and even though her huge eyes were looking straight at us, it did not seem as though she saw us. A shiver of more than fear ran down my spine.

"Yes, we will look after her," Papa said gently to his sister.

Oh, Gerritt! I can hear the angels singing!" Tante Annette's eyes lifted toward the ceiling.

My father was cradling her in his arms. I could see tears brimming over and running down his cheeks.

I stood in the middle of that room and was struck with absolute clarity what a horrible life they had been living. Cut off from the rest of the world, they had literally starved to death.

"She is gone," Papa murmured. "We arrived just in time to see her die."

A moan from the corner drew his attention to my cousin. With a gigantic stride, he was lifting her into his arms and holding her tightly against her chest.

"Tokie, come! Bring the parcel! We have to take her back to Mama!"

Now it was daylight. Our boat could more readily be seen from any guards watching for unusual traffic on the river.

"Give her a little bread. No meat!" Papa instructed. He took his position and pushed out into the water.

"The poor dear," Mama said rising from the bed. "She came too late."

For two days after we had managed to bring Willemina home by boat, miraculously passing by all the checkpoints unchallenged, my mama had tried to nurse my cousin back to health again.

Trying to get her to drink hot tea, and feeding her spoonfuls of meat broth did not help. Every day, little Willemina became weaker and on the third day, she died.

So, her body was wrapped up completely and Mama carried her out on the street and gently lay her by the front step.

We could hear the death wagon, as we called it, coming up the Hoogstraat. Every day, the two big black horses went up and down the streets of Werkendam, gathering up those that had died.

The past winter, it had hardly ever been a day that the wagon was not stacked with bodies. Diphtheria and typhoid had swept through our wretched town and death claimed many of the elderly and weak. Several old men toiled daily to dig the graves and bury the bodies. There was no funeral, no gathering of relatives and friends. There were simply too many dead.

I saw the long, low buildings on the horizon, surrounded by two barbed wire fences and spaced all along the fence at intervals and at the four corners, guardhouses on stilts giving the armed soldiers a good view of anyone approaching. A water-filled moat divided the fences.

But the road I was on led right past the main entrance. On my mission to find food, I had decided to try going on further east and this road led me right past Konzentrationslager Herzogenbosch, the German camp where Dutch and Belgium prisoners were incarcerated. And Jews.

For there were many tales that reached our ears about this infamous prison. Sometimes it was whispered that every so often, train loads of prisoners were transported into Germany, never to be heard from again. Other times, there were reports of volleys of gunshots coming from inside the grim fences. Even now, I could see a tall brick chimney poking up into the sky, gray smoke drifting up and trailing away downwind.

As crazy as it may sound, curiosity drew me closer and I looked into the prison yard through the main gates.

I saw a group of men, heads shaved and wearing striped prison suits, being beaten by a screaming guard.

Then, I was being screamed at. "You little tramp! Get moving out of here before we push you inside!" The guard beside the gate was yelling at me and brandishing his rifle.

I sprinted down the road, away from the awfulness of that place. I believed everything I had ever heard about this place called Vught. For I realized that what I had seen was just a very small portion of what really was happening inside that place worse than nightmares. Later, when I met Corrie ten Boom, the famous and courageous Christian woman, I learned that after her arrest, she had been in that very camp for a short time.

But now, all I wanted was to get far away from that place

of misery and death. I decided right then I would return home some other way.

There were other vivid reminders of what was happening to Holland during the occupation by the Germans.

A small village not far from us was called Widows' Town. Someone in that town, probably a Dutch resistance fighter, had killed a German soldier. In retaliation, the Germans had killed all the males in that town, even the baby boys.

So, we lived in constant fear of the unknown. As year after year passed and the broadcasts from England announced more and more fierce fighting between the Allies and the Germans, hope surged, only to die back down once more. Papa still listened to our radio, but it was as though, for me, there was no other life. I could no longer imagine anything else except scrounging for food, trying to stay warm and clothed and the constant presence of the German soldiers, reminding us daily that we were in their power.

CHAPTER FIVE

FREEDOM?

"We will wait until this evening to eat them," Mama decided as she lifted a hot, smoking olie bollen, the Dutch name for doughnuts, from the oil.

All of us children watched as another plump doughnut joined the few that were already removed from the hot oil.

My little sisters, Jurriana, Jenneke, and Johanna were all eyes. Doughnuts were something they could not even remember! But they sure smelled delicious!

Reitze and I remembered in the prewar days about Dutch doughnuts. The dough had to rise first, and then they were dropped into the hot oil, there to turn a delicious brown and give out the most delectable aroma.

My mind was busy. How could I manage to take several doughnuts before I left on my excursion outside. I did not want to tell Mama about my planned trip, for what I did, I kept secret.

For another thirty minutes, we were engrossed in the kitchen activities. The little girls ran about, excited over the prospect of something new and delicious to eat. It would make an exciting change from our plain fare of boiled grain and occasionally some dry bread.

It had been Papa who had brought the oil home on one of his secret visits to see us. Occasionally, the black market provided treats and items that had not been available for the last several years of the war.

He had brought more than just oil home. He had told us about the nervous German army and how they were committing more atrocious deeds than before. "They know the Allies are pushing back the Germans. From Russia, the armies are driving the Germans back into their own country, and from the west, the British, Canadians and Americans are pushing hard to break the hold of the German army. They are getting scared."

Papa looked both grim and glad. I knew that he had heard of some very gruesome happenings against our countrymen. The Dutch Resistance movement was beginning a renewed effort to help the Allies all they could.

The smell of the doughnuts, temporarily made me forget the war. Inside our house, we were a family once again, even if Papa was gone.

"Baby Gerrit has fallen off the sofa!" Jurriana yelled to Mama from the other room.

The two little girls and Mama rushed in to see what had happened.

In the midst of the confusion, the girls fussing, the baby crying and Mama comforting her little son, I was able to slip two doughnuts into my pocket when Reitze wasn't looking.

I could see my breath in the frosty air outside, but the doughnuts were warm in my right hand. As soon as I was around the corner, I bit into the first doughnut and devoured it. The second one followed right on the heels of the first, if doughnuts have heels.

They made a warm, comforting lump in my stomach. But I felt disappointed in the taste. There was something different about these doughnuts. I had remembered eating the prewar doughnuts and they had tasted better. Not so oily.

Before curfew at six o'clock, I always tried to walk around in Werkendam, spying out any potential place where I might be able to get food after dark. There were fewer chickens, less cows, and food was becoming more and more scarce. I often had to scrounge further and further away from our town in order to find food. But no matter where I went, food was getting very difficult to find.

I knew Papa was working harder to find food for his growing family. Since Gerrit, named after his daddy, had joined our family, it was a daily struggle to provide food for all of us.

I was on the far side of town, when I felt my stomach begin to churn. Groaning, I bent over, holding my middle.

As the attack continued, I sat on the front steps of a vacant building. I took deep breaths as my roiling stomach protested.

"Oh, why did I eat those doughnuts?" I groaned to myself. It felt as though there was a war going on inside of me. As cold as it was, I felt myself break into a sweat.

I sat there, gasping deep breaths of cold air, and clutching my stomach for a long time. Spasms of pain tore through my body until I even lay face down on the concrete step, trying to get some relief.

Darkness had stalked in between the rows of houses before I was finally able to take my tortured and wretched body slowly home. I drug my klompen over the cobblestones, barely able to lift my feet.

My mind seemed to dumb down and I was vaguely aware of a sensation of something wet running down my legs. I did not care. All I wanted was to get home and collapse in my bed.

"There he is!" Mama looked up from the table. "Tokie, you didn't eat any of the olie bollen, did you?" Then, her brows furrowed as she looked intently at my face.

"I can see you did," Concern was mixed in with exasperation. "You are sick."

From the dark corner, I heard Papa. "This time, your crime has punished you. I came back to warn no one to use anything that was cooked in the oil, for the man who sold the oil had mixed motor oil in with the cooking oil. He was found out, and beaten.

"I came home to warn Mama and the family. She told me that, thankfully, no one had eaten any. They were saving them for this evening." He chuckled, but it was not a chuckle that had any mirth in it.

"Eew! Something stinks!" Jenneke held her nose.

I was so weak, I fell onto the sofa.

"Get away!" Reitze yelled. "Papa, he has diareaha!"

I was in disgrace all the next day. Mama was upset with me because I had snitched the doughnuts and my brother refused to sleep in the same bed with me. Papa had forced me to go outside and wash, and I think he barely allowed Mama to warm the water I had to use.

I was still so weak from my upset stomach that I could barely wash, but I knew better than to go inside before the odorous task was done.

"Tokie, keep out of trouble," Papa warned me before he left the house. "You are becoming so independent it is not only dangerous for us, it is making you into a rebel."

I said nothing. His words rankled deep inside my head and even though I knew what he said was true, I did not care. I was becoming accustomed to making my own way, taking my own way and deciding what I would do and what I would not do.

"Victory!"

"Freedom!"

It was on a Saturday when the Canadian troops came rolling into our town, horns blaring, and freed us from the Germans.

True, the German forces had already fled several days before, and the town was rife with rumors, but it was not until May the 5th, 1945, that we really knew for sure that we were free.

People streamed from their houses, welcoming the Canadians. Dutch flags, hidden during the occupation, flew from the second story windows, and there was a sense of exhilaration that threw even the most staid and dignified Dutchman into a state of gladness and joy.

"Papa can come home!" Mama cried out joyfully, tears running down her cheeks.

App and I burst out into the streets and joined the happy throng. Bells were ringing, the noise of the welcoming throng surged up from the streets and shouts of pure joy echoed everywhere. Someone began to sing our national anthem, and soon, our entire village was ringing with the Wilhelmus.

"The Queen can come home!"

"We will have food to eat!"

As soon as someone thought of something that could now begin again, it was shouted out to all the world.

The Canadians tossed chocolate candy into the crowds, and we children scrambled and fought on the streets for the treats.

Then, the airplanes began flying overhead, leaving trails of smoke across our skies. They did ariel maneuvers, celebrating the victory we all were now a part of. Hidden radios blared with speeches, and I heard the voice of Winston Churchill in London, celebrating with the cheering crowds. We were delirious with joy.

I ran around the corner and then stopped suddenly.

The old pastor of the Reformed Lutheran Church, with tears streaming down his face, was clambering laboriously up the pile of rubble that had once been the church building. The steeple lay half buried among the pile of stones.

In his hand, the pastor carried the Dutch flag, tied to a stick. He waved it triumphantly, even though he could hardly climb up the pile of rubbish.

At the top, he plunged the stick into the between two stones and as it waved slightly in the breeze, the pastor sank down onto his knees.

"They can take away the stone building, but we have a house not made with hands! There is still victory in Jesus!" His voice trembled with his emotion, but once more he rallied and cried out, "Victory in Jesus!"

The echoes of the jubilant crowds were still resounding on the main street. The cries of "Freedom" were ringing out everywhere. But, somehow, as godless as I was as a boy, something about the scene before me struck a deep cord in my soul. I was witnessing something holy.

"Please have mercy!"

I heard the shrill scream of a girl spread through the crowd in front of the town hall.

"I am sorry! No! No!"

I pushed my way through the crowd until I could see.

There on the porch of the town hall was a small group of girls, fear-filled eyes running over the crowd, looking for a compassionate face.

"Ask the Germans now to help you! They are gone, or dead,

and now it is your turn!" Words and cries were flung at the helpless girls like so many stones.

"You need not to ask for mercy from us! You ask God for mercy!" An old woman cried out from the crowd, her face twisted with hatred.

I knew who those girls were. I had seen some of them at the officer's Christmas party, laughing and dancing and drinking. They had looked pretty to me then, all smiles and shining faces.

The contrast now was enormous. Their hair hung down over their faces and mud was splattered on some of them.

"Here comes another one!" Someone cried, and I saw another girl pushed through the crowd. Two energetic middle-aged women, scissors in hand, were shearing the girls and their long hair, writhing down over their shoulders, fell to the floor of the porch.

"If you loved the Germans, then here!" A deacon from one of the churches dipped a paint brush into a pail of white paint and painted the hated swastika on their now bald heads.

Even though there were a few protests from some in the crowd, the majority of the people were determined to vent their suppressed anger onto someone. Jeers and cries of "Shame! Shame!" now filled the streets that earlier had rung with the heady cries of "Freedom!" and "Victory!"

The heady feeling of victory and freedom had given way to retaliation and punishment. Anyone who had collaborated with the Germans was flushed out of hiding and if not jailed, made to feel the full brunt of their misdeeds. Old scores were settled and as Papa and the other men in hiding came home, they were able to identify even more people who had supported the puppet rulers.

Even as a young thirteen year old boy, I was amazed by the vindictiveness and anger of my fellow countrymen. Every day brought news of what the liberators and the Dutch people were doing to any Germans that were caught in our country.

As news spread of the horrible conditions in the concentration camps, the people literally gnashed their teeth and dragged any

Germans onto the street where the survivors smashed them to death with their wooden shoes.

And in my mind, there was a new problem. Freedom from occupying forces did not solve all the problems. It should be that now that we were free, we should work together to get our lives back in order again and learn to live peaceably among ourselves.

Instead, there was a new wave of bickering and hate that swept over our country. We seemed not much different inside than what we had been before. Something inside of me cried out against the injustice of life. I felt disillusionment sweep over me.

Chapter Six

REBEL

D odging a bad spot in the road, Papa drove the truck out of our village, headed for the countryside.

"When can I drive the truck?" I yelled over the noise of the army vehicle, for my father had bought it from the Allies before they left our area.

"Humph!" was all my father answered.

Like teen-aged boys everywhere, I was fascinated by automobiles. After the war, only the wealthy had cars and trucks, and even though our truck was rather old and beat up, I had a driving ambition to learn how to drive it.

Going along at a moderate speed, I watched as my father shifted from one gear to the next, either shifting to a lower gear when the road was rough, or shifting to a higher gear when the road was smooth. I took my right arm and made shifting motions with it, trying to do it smoothly, like Papa did.

"What a terrible waste!" Papa said loudly, shaking his head. I looked up and saw a field filled with holes where bombs had been dropped and where debris from fallen airplanes littered the ground.

"No one can plant in fields like that! It will take a long time for our country to recover from our terrible experience!" I sensed my father's anger.

"Here it is," Papa said as he shifted into low and we entered the yard of a farm.

The farmyard was located right next to the dike and when Papa stopped the truck, he pulled the hand brake up for the yard sloped away from the dike toward the buildings.

"I hope they really do have potatoes. I can get a good price for potatoes in town." Papa shut off the engine and opened the door.

I started to open my side door, then looking at the gear shift, I decided to stay inside the truck. It would be boring to go inside and listen to the grown ups haggle about the price of potatoes.

"Tokie!" Papa frowned at me, "now don't go messing with anything!" He seemed to deliberate about something, then warned me, "Don't touch the gear shift!"

"Oh, no, Papa," I said as convincingly as a thirteen year old boy could. I gazed out the window toward the peaceful farmyard scene to show I was not interested in anything inside the truck.

The barn was opposite the house and I wondered if the potatoes were stored in a bin there somewhere. Maybe Papa would let me drive the truck over there. It would be simple, for the truck was already facing the barn.

I pretended to start the engine, looked at the gear shift, and made a motion above the knob, just like it should be done.

I would go slowly, of course, since the distance would be short. Just a few yards, and then I would step on the brake, and there, the truck would be conveniently parked close to where we would load the potatoes.

Time went on, and no one came out of the house.

I slipped across the seat and sat behind the steering wheel. I gave the wheel a few experimental turns and felt a slight response from the front wheels. I tugged harder.

I placed my hand on the gear shift. It felt tight and secure. The hand brake was right next to it, so I slid my hand up and down the shaft.

I would do it! It took me only a moment to decide, and as quick as the thought came to me, I pushed in the clutch, started the engine, and pushed the gas pedal.

The motor hummed smoothly. I felt the delightful sensation of power surging through me.

I jiggled the gear shift and it moved easily. The diagram on top of the shift helped, for I pushed it toward the R. I knew enough English that yes, R meant race, and that would mean to go forward.

As soon as the gear had moved into R, I released the hand brake and pressed the gas, gunning the motor. Now, I released the clutch, and with a roar, the truck went backwards, the motor roaring and the tires screeching!

I was too startled to even think what I should do! I frantically steered the roaring truck, in my excitement pushing the gas pedal right to the floorboards!

There was a terrific crash and the jolt knocked both my feet from the pedals, and feeling as though I had hit a stone wall, I was thrown against the steering column, my face smashing against the horn.

Then, for only a moment, there was silence.

I was gingerly moving away from the steering wheel when I heard a high pitched scream, "The Germans are back! They have bombed the house!"

For a few minutes, there was pandemonium. I saw my father's face, terrible in rage, outside the truck and then, opening the door, he pulled me out and without bothering to check if I was hurt, he struck my back and sent me reeling away from the truck.

The farm woman was screaming and wringing her hands in horror.

When Papa finally released me, I could barely believe my eyes.

The rear of the truck had crashed into the corner of the house, pushing in the brick wall and a gaping hole revealed the inside of the house!

The back of the truck was crumpled and the tail gate lay on top of a pile of bricks. Inside, I could see broken dishes scattered across the floor and a china cabinet turned over.

This accident, I knew, was going to be costly. Not only for repairing the truck, or even worse, all the time and money to repair the farm house, but also for me.

"Now straight to bed!" Papa was breathing heavily as he threw the paddle into the corner of the room.

My bottom stung from my punishment, and I stomped up the steep stairs to my room.

All the way home, my father had been telling me what a wayward and wicked son I was.

"I tell you to stay in at night, and the next morning, I find out you were gone for hours. Whatever I say means nothing to you!" His voice fumed as we drove the damaged truck home.

"I found food for the family while you were gone," I defended myself angrily. "Reitze did nothing and you were gone, so I had to provide. You didn't yell at me then!"

My father's face turned red. "The war is over! Now I am at home and you are going to listen to me! Do you hear?

"You are running wild and undisciplined! You are headed for ruin!" I heard a note of desperation in his voice.

I shrugged my shoulder and looked out the window. I pretended not to care.

So, it had been no surprise when we reached home that my father spanked me. I was getting used to these incidents since he had moved home.

At first, I had thought my father was proud of how I had managed to escape from all my escapades during the war, and perhaps he had been. But now, I was a threat to his authority, and I knew he was determined to control me.

In bed, as reflected on life, I decided that there was no sense to anything anymore. I almost longed for the days of German occupation, for then, at least the enemy had been outside our house, and my wits had been able to outsmart them for the five years they had been in our country. Even the memory of hunger and want was fading compared to the deep unrest that I felt inside of me.

Our village felt small and confining. Working for my father in his oil business held no prospects of excitement. Taking the pushcart of oil cans from place to place to sell the oil to the customers was hard and unrewarding work.

I wanted excitement! I wanted to test my skills and broaden my horizons! I wanted away, out of this house and from my father's continual efforts to control and constrict my independent nature!

"Hey, Oil Man! You make a pretty good horse!"

I pretended not to hear the taunts and laughter of my school mates. I pushed hard against the handles of the oil cart.

"Is it oil today and flour tomorrow?" I heard the disdain in Leendert's voice.

Rage boiled up inside of me. I stopped the cart and straightened up, clenching my fists.

Leendert watched me warily, his friends standing on either side of him.

I knew I was outnumbered. "Shut up!" I hissed, red hot with anger.

"Aww, keep your hat on," Leendert tried to save the situation. "You just have to work to keep yourself out of trouble. It is good for you."

I lifted the wooden handles and began to push the cart away from them, but inside, I was still seething.

The words of my classmate smarted. "Work to keep yourself out of trouble." Those were the exact words Papa used whenever I complained about the extra work he piled on me.

"But Reitze studies hard and is not continually in trouble," Papa reminded me sternly when I boldly asked why I was the only one that had to do the hard manual labor.

"Be like Reitze! See how Reitze studies!" My voice had risen in anger. "I am not Reitze and can never be like him! I don't want to be like Reitze, always afraid of doing anything daring or ever having any fun! I am me, Tom!"

My outburst brought no results. It only seemed to alienate myself further from my family.

In the next few years, I grew restive and sullen at home. I made friends with the boys from the village who were not afraid to try out new and dangerous things, and we terrorized many of the townspeople.

"Gerrit, no!" I heard my mother say firmly, "I will not agree to anyone taking Tokie to that, that detention place! He will learn more wicked ways there than he already knows here!"

"But," my father's voice came clearly to me from my hiding place. "He..."

Mama's voice rose several decibels. She did not care if the entire neighborhood could hear her. "You can not send your own son away! I know he is into all kinds of mischief and trouble, but he is your own flesh and blood!

"We were able to stay alive all during the war and you know Tokie was the one who often brought us food when there was nothing in the house." I could hear the determination in my mother's voice, and yet, I could also hear the tears that were threatening to spill down over her cheeks.

"I have made the arrangements," Papa tried to defend himself. "The guards are outside, waiting. Plus, the elders from the town are insisting we do something! We can't let this go on, Moeder!"

"I don't care if the guards are waiting or not. I had a talk with Tokie and as soon as he is seventeen, he will join the Armed Forces! They will train him and provide the discipline he needs."

From my hiding place in the closet, I could hear every word plainly. I scrunched behind the clothes and waited to hear the outcome.

I had not realized that Papa had actually put his threats into action. More than once he had yelled at me, "You are headed for reform school!"

Now there were guards outside, ready to "escort" me to the reformatory! I did not even dare try to escape.

It had been while Mama was talking to me that we had heard footsteps outside. She had not told me that Papa was out, getting the guards to take me. She had just begun talking about signing up with the army when suddenly, she had stood up, and said hoarsely, "They are here!" and pushed me into the clothes closet.

As my parents argued about my fate, I felt the familiar frustration rise up inside me again. I was so trapped! If only I could find complete freedom!

The armed forces sounded like a good alternative to life at home in a pokey old village. Anything would be better that living in Werkendam!

Well, not anything. I did not want to go to reform school, for we all heard tales of the brutality of the guards and how renegades were beaten into submission.

The war had seemed to bring about a huge increase of hoodlums, much like myself who had escaped the war years only to find themselves bored and restless during the reconstruction. Some had lost their families and had become bitter and disillusioned. Others, like myself, felt the change in the air and wanted to be a part of it. Yes, there were many casualties of war that did not end in death.

"O.K. You win!" My father finally said. "But he will keep out of trouble until he is in the army or next time, I will not yield!"

Then, after a pause, he said, "I don't know what to tell the waiting men."

"Never mind," Mama's voice was triumphant. "I will tell them. No son of mine is going to that reform school." Our small house shook as she slammed the front door shut.

In the following year, I really tried to stay out of trouble. I was rarely at home, though, for our house was crowded with my siblings, and when everyone was at home, there were ten all gathered under one roof.

My father's appliance repair business prospered and we helped him. The village slowly began to recover from the war and tradesmen brought goods from all over the world on the canal boats.

The day I signed up for the armed forces brought me into a completely different world. I was thrust into a regimen of order and training that both challenged me and brought meaning into my life. I was able to explore new horizons and felt I had found the answers to living. Holland was in reconstruction and I was a part of it now.

CHAPTER SEVEN

NEW LIFE

I guided the Massey Ferguson tractor over the flat field, harrowing the soil in preparation for planting. In the next field, Richard, my boss, was running the potato plow, creating furrows in readiness for planting the seed potatoes, for which Newfoundland was famous.

The tractor engine ran smoothly in a monotonous regularity. The warm spring sunshine felt good after the winter cold. I could almost imagine myself back in Holland out here in the fields, except I was not used to seeing fences separate the pastures from the fields. Here, there were no canals, so the farmers had to build miles of fences to keep their livestock in their fields.

There was something else different, though it was hard to tell what it really was. Just a difference in the air, perhaps.

I remembered that when I had first arrived on the shores of Canada in Halifax, I had been amazed at the hustle and bustle of the seaport city. Everything seemed louder, bigger, and even the people seemed to be different. They talked more and louder, laughing and bustling about. I had imagined it to be like Amsterdam, but the West really was different, more alive.

As I bounced over the plowed field, I had plenty of time to think back over the past several years.

I had been in the Dutch Armed Forces for only several years until once more, I had felt restricted and held back by all the orders and rules. Even though I had learned a lot of discipline that I knew was good for me, I wanted to experience something more. Life should have more excitement.

My idea to immigrate to Canada had sprung to life when I heard that the northern American country was accepting European immigrants. The soldiers in the army would often talk about the better life that surely must await anyone ambitious.

All of Europe was still wallowing in the postwar efforts and life was difficult for many people. Dead end jobs and back breaking labor, working long hours for only a mere pittance, held no romance for me.

"You are not going to Canada!" My father had been aghast at

the very idea. "To a foreign country where we would never see you again or hear from you! Absolutely not!"

I had been at home for a weekend when I had first mentioned my interest to immigrate.

"Dad! There are hundreds of men immigrating! There is a new life over there! A better life!" I had once more felt confined by demands on my life.

"A better life? A lawless life of cut throats and outlaws! With your 'adventurous spirit' and recklessness, you will be in prison in no time with no one to watch over you." He had shaken his head until his glasses slid down on his nose.

"I am a man now! I am 23 years old! Do you want me to stay here, getting paid some paltry sum digging ditches? There is money to be made in Canada! An easier life!" I had become excited just talking about it.

"Tokie!" Mama had joined in, "how can you think of leaving your family and relatives? This is your life! Werkendam is your home!"

But I had persisted even in spite of all the obstacles in front of me. In fact, when I had gone to withdraw my measly savings from my bank account, I had learned that my father had already been there and withdrew everything. I had been very upset then that I had ever consented to having a joint account with my parents. But then, it had been too late.

Even, after I had spoken to the army official who was to oversee my release and immigration papers, I had been blocked once more by my father.

"I'm sorry, Tom. You do not have permission to go. Your father has been here and made it impossible for you to leave."

I had stormed out and gone to my barracks, seething with anger and determination.

Finally, after weeks of working with army officials, I had been able to sail across the ocean toward the West. My last visit home had not been a happy one. My young siblings had been crying along with my mother and my father and the older ones had been stern and silent.

I reached the end of the field and turned the tractor around. The freshly harrowed soil shone darkly in the sunshine, and overhead the sea gulls wheeled and cried shrilly before settling themselves on the soil, hunting for grubs.

I had been with Richard and Sally Peterson for a two months now, working on their farm. I had not found the transition from Holland an easy one to make.

First, there was the language barrier. I landed on the shores of Canada knowing hardly anything more than, yes, no, girl, and money. Those words did not get me far in finding a job.

If it had not been for other Dutch people, I would have really been lost. Someone had found me this job with the Petersons, and here I was, stuck in another boring, dead-end job. The $40 I was paid a month was not going to make me rich soon. I stayed in their upstairs as a hired man, but mostly what I was gaining was a window into the complexities of the English language.

I had signed a paper, stating I would work for the farming couple for a year. Now, the year stretched ahead of me like an unending drudgery of hard work. Once more, I felt the constrictions that wanted to choke me sometimes.

I looked over at Richard as he worked steadily in the field next to me. His face had a permanent frown and he hardly ever looked happy.

I knew he blamed his wife for most of his unhappiness. Sally sure wasn't happy. She nagged and nattered all the time we were in the house, her words making no sense to me, but the tone of voice and her whine told me all I needed to know.

Outside, Richard would mumble and complain to me about his wife. As I began to pick up more and more English words, I soon learned that whenever he would talk about his wife to me, he would call her, "The old hag."

Now learning that had taken me into, "hot water", as they say in English.

One day, Richard had sent me to the house to ask Sally for water to take along to the field.

Sally had been in the kitchen, her back towards me, working at the sink. I had wanted to get her attention, for she had not heard me coming into the house. To say "Sally" seemed unmannerly and rude, so I did the best I could.

"Excuse me, hag!" I said in a pleasant voice. "Richard say need water for field to take."

As Mrs. Sally had turned to face me, I had seen her face turn from shock to a dreadful purple. Then, to my alarm, she had grabbed a bread knife from the counter and shrieking a stream of incomprehensible words at me, she had lunged toward me. I could still see that shining knife blade pointed straight at me.

That had been a disastrous day. When I had tried to tell Mr. Richard what had happened, all my English had turned to garble.

"Slow down, Tom! What did you do?"

We had been out by the barn, and as soon as I had seen Mrs. Sally come screaming around the corner, I had fled.

But had I peeped around the corner of the barn and when Mr. Richard had burst out into a loud laugh and Mrs. Sally had lunged toward him, I had not been sure what was going to happen.

"You dumb guy!" Mr. Richard had said, shaking his head. "You got us both into 'hot water'!"

All of these incidents kept tumbling over and over in my head as I spent hours on the tractor. Was this all there was to life in Canada?

"Life in the cities are much different, Tom," a Dutchman I had befriended told me. "Not like out here in the country."

"Then why are you here?" I asked curiously.

"I have a family," he reasoned. "For my wife and children, it is a good place. We have small house, place to grow food. For us, it is good.

"Is important, though, to know English. Must speak the language!"

His words seemed to burn inside my mind. For the next several days, I could think of nothing else.

Life with the Petersons continued to deteriorate. My English continued to improve, but now I realized that I must learn the meanings of innocent sounding words and not use any words unless I was sure that I knew just what they meant.

There was a dangerous gleam in Mrs. Sally's eyes and more than once, Mr. Richard referred to his wife as "crazy". It did not take much to convince me that she was mentally imbalanced.

So, I left. Took my few belongings and what little money I had and bought a train ticket for Hamilton, Ontario.

"Is a big city, with lots of work," my Dutch friend had told me when I had quizzed him where I should go.

That bewildering big city was filled with immigrants looking for work. For a while, I had found some small jobs with the blessings of a Dutch Reformed elder, but he was so domineering and bossy that I felt I was back home in Werkendam with my father again.

"Needing workers for the cotton mill," I heard on the street one day. I joined the crowd of hopeful workers and stood patiently inline for hours.

"If you are not a trained spinner or a qualified spinning machine mechanic, go home!" The words blared out from a loud speaker. "We are only hiring experienced workers!"

I raised my arm and began shouting, "I mechanic! I spinner! I experience!" Wading through the crowd, I rushed toward the entrance.

Here, in the office, there was an amazing amount of commotion. The weary man who had led me inside after my declaration that I was experienced asked me a lot of questions that I did not understand but I kept nodding my head and saying, "I experience in the field," whenever he asked me a question. He finally shrugged and led me into the factory room.

The noise inside was deafening from the scores of machines

spinning the cotton into thread. A man led me to an enormous machine that was clacking away under the direction of a middle aged woman who looked suspiciously at me.

"Keep the machine in order!" My guide shouted at me.

I nodded in what I hoped was an experienced nod and looked inquiringly at the machine in front of me. I had not the slightest idea what the machine was doing, much less how it worked.

"Your turn!" the lady shouted at me in English, motioning to the front of the machine where she had been standing, keeping an eagle eye on the action in front of her.

I smiled broadly and took her place. I looked intently at what was happening, but I had no idea what I should be watching for.

Then, there was a whirr, and one of the spools seemed to rise up from its spindle.

There was a shriek from behind me and the woman dashed past my station and pushed the spindle back down.

A torrent of words flowed over my head, and to my surprise, I could understand them!

Then, it dawned on me she was speaking Dutch! I was called all the familiar names I had heard addressed to me for years. Dunderhead, dumb, no nothing, all of them.

"But, but what am I supposed to be watching for?" I finally stammered in my mother tongue.

"You are from Holland! My name is Julia!" Suddenly, I was a friend.

If it had not been for Julia taking me under her training, I am sure I would have been fired the second day. She scolded me for putting too much oil in the machine when I "maintained" it and schooled me what to watch for.

"I could not believe they hired you when you first came," she told me only a week later. "You knew nothing about spinning. How did you get in?"

I smiled at her, "Sometimes if you just go ahead and do something, it works out."

I soon worked by myself on the night shift. I slept through

the morning hours and roamed the city in the afternoon and evening, learning how to survive in a huge city.

"What happens to the clothes no one picks up?" I asked in my new English. I had gone into a laundry and dry cleaning shop and stared in amazement at the racks of clothes hanging in the back.

"After a month, we sell them." The owner shrugged his shoulders. "But we still have way too many."

The wheels of commerce began to slowly revolve in my brain.

"How much dollars you want for that rack?" I asked pointing to the last row.

"Take the two rows for $200. I need the space."

My mind was now spinning rapidly. "Yes! I come tonight at five o'clock and give you the money and take the clothes."

Just down the block was a used car dealer. My fascination with automobiles had not ended, even after the disaster with my father's truck. I knew all the different makes, the models, and the prices.

"You ready to buy, Tom?" The salesman was used to seeing me hang around the car lot.

"Yes," I replied smoothly. "Today, I put to test this car."

When he saw I was not joking, he said seriously, "Let me get the key."

He showed me how the car worked, and I slowly drove out of the yard. My months on the tractor had taught me a lot about driving.

"Around the block, I go," I yelled. "If I like, I buy."

I must have sounded convincing, because he just waved his hand.

Immediately, I went to the dry cleaning shop, paid the $200 and loaded the car with the clothes. Then, I sped out of the city.

I knew just where to go. One of my room mates worked in the tobacco fields and he had told me that newly-arrived immigrants swarmed in to do a job where they could learn by example and did not need to know English.

The workers were just coming out of the fields when I arrived. I opened the car doors, spread out the nice suits and clothes on the hood, the trunk and draped them over the open doors.

"Clothes for to sell!" I yelled, pointing to my wares.

It worked. I sold the good quality clothes all evening until I had sold all of them.

Before I went to work at the spinning factory, I counted my money. I could hardly believe it! I had made over a thousand dollars in one night!

But the car! I knew I was in trouble as soon as I drove into the car lot.

"You are crazy! I reported you to the police!" Tony's voice hit me as soon as I drove in.

I slowly opened the door and bending over in an awkward position, I began groaning.

"Oh, such a pain. Hospital in the night," I lied.

Then, assuming to straighten up, I said loudly, "I buy car for $800. You sell to me?" I pulled out my roll of money.

Tony's salesman nature took over. "I will call the police and tell them it is a mistake. Yes, for $800 you can buy the car."

So, I bought the old car and began tracking down other laundry and dry cleaning shops. They were all eager to get rid of the clothing and I found that there was a ready market for the clothes from the immigrants. Many of the young men and women wanted to buy the Canadian clothes and leave any vestige of their homelands behind them, so my wares were in a great demand.

Even though the work in the factory was boring, it seemed as though I was given a new lease on life. I expanded my enterprises and did remarkably well.

I worked in the north in the lumber camps for a year, but I did not like doing that. That summer I learned all about black flies and mosquitoes. In the winter, it was so cold that there were days we could not work the horses, for fear their lungs would freeze.

After an accident where I cut my leg with an ax, I managed to get back to Hamilton, where I eventually bought a restaurant. There, I was bested by the owner, who told me what a successful business he had, when in reality, I could barely make the payments, much less make a living.

Such was my early life in Canada. Learning English, getting by with my own wits, taking advantage of other people and being taken advantage of. There were times when I thought I was happy, but in reality, I was still searching for something more. Something that was exciting and would continue to inspire me for the rest of my life.

Then, I thought I found it.

CHAPTER EIGHT

THE REASON

I hunched up my shoulders against the cold and trudged on, oblivious to the roaring traffic approaching the Jacque Cartier Bridge in downtown Montreal. The speeding cars and blowing horns were all a part of the living nightmare that surrounded me.

Bits of snow stung my cheeks and the cold made my eyes water in the early darkness of the winter evening. At least, I guessed it was the cold that made the tears wet my cheeks.

The pedestrian walk was divided from the traffic lanes and I walked onto the bridge for several yards before stopping and staring down into the darkness below. The metal guard rail was cold and unforgiving, and I leaned against the side, my mind in a whirl.

Tonight, I was not drunk. I was not high on drugs. I was coldly sober. My memories of the past several years flooded through me with startling clarity. How vividly I recalled my past life. Too vividly.

When I first had met Tina, who worked as a waitress in the restaurant I had just bought, I had been attracted by her lively spirit and attractive face. I had grown to love her, and when the restaurant begun to prosper with her unfailing hard work and enthusiasm, I had proposed to her.

Then, I had thought that life was finally in my hands. A successful business, a lovely wife and all of my future had been before me. I had thought I was no longer the Dutch nobody from Holland, but then, I had been sure that I had been an important person with my own destiny in my own hands!

I had even gone back to Werkendam for awhile, and there it had been as usual, everyone still grubbing along just to make a living. I had gladly escaped back to Canada, settling in Montreal.

Now, on the bridge, in the dead of winter, my hopelessness wanted to wash over me. Why, oh, why had I ever allowed myself to sink to this level?

I was a complete failure. My wife had left me, taking our two children with her. I had lost our house, my business and everything I owned. I was a street person, living from hand to mouth, begging for food, for money, for anything I could get. I joined the long lines at soup kitchens, getting one hot meal a day. If I could, I would spend the night in homeless shelters, trying to stay warm. In the summer, I slept anywhere, sleeping off drunken stupors or completely stoned from drugs.

Suddenly, tonight, it all seemed too much. I shook my head wearily as I thought back to my childhood in Werkendam. The senselessness of the war, the constant struggle to find food and stay clothes, the hatred that had grown inside against the Germans and then the struggle between myself and my father.

Every time I had thought I would find happiness and fulfillment for my life, my hopes had been dashed. I remembered how I had thought when I joined the army that life would now take on new meaning and how quickly I had become bored with being a soldier in training. Then, my life in Canada had taken on new meaning as I had become successful.

At first, my marriage to Tina had been wonderful. I had loved her very much, but as I had spiraled downwards into drinking and drug use, I had lost her love and respect. I had lost everything.

I studied the darkness below me. The cold began to seep through my coat and I could feel my feet began to get numb.

The river was down below. But I was not over the water. I was standing above the concrete that lined the river bank.

I knew this part of the bridge very well. I had often seen it in the daylight, so now, I did not need any light in order to see what lay down there in the darkness.

No place to go. My life ruined before I was even forty. I knew I looked older, for my decadent lifestyle had aged me prematurely. "Your hands shake like an old man's," Tina told me before she left. "You are ruining your life. I refuse to let you ruin my life, too."

"Please, don't go!" I had pled with her. "I will stay away from the bars and druggies! Promise!"

"Tom, I have heard those promises for more years than I want to remember. Broken promises, that is all I hear anymore. You are not even fit to argue with me." She had left. Now, he was all alone.

Alone with his memories. Alone with the darkness growing larger and larger inside him until it opened its mouth and tugged at him. "Throw yourself over the edge and end it all! You will die instantly! No more cold, no more loneliness!" The monster in his brain beckoned seductively.

My breath came in shorter gasps. I reached out and touched the cold steel of the railing. My muscles tensed.

"Go! Go!" Voices shrieked inside my head.

Into the clamor of my brain, I heard a soft voice, "Come! Come unto Me, all you who are weary!"

Shaking my head in disbelief, I lifted my head. Who had spoken to me?

"Come! Come to me!"

"Go! Go on! Jump!" The words were screaming in my consciousness.

"Come! Come to Me! You are weary, you are tired. Come now to Me!"

I shook my head in disbelief. Where were those words coming from? Who was saying them?

"What about your children? What will Tina have to tell them? 'Your father killed himself. You have no father.'" The voice kept on.

"Do you really want to die? What will happen to your soul? There is a part of you that never dies. What will happen once your body is no longer breathing?" Questions kept popping into my mind.

I was no longer sure if I was speaking to myself, or if the voice was still speaking. I could still hear the demonic voice yelling, "Go on! End all this misery and throw yourself over the rail." But that voice seemed farther away.

Then, I felt a strange emotion come over me. It was as though Someone was standing beside me. Someone saying, "Come!"

Like a flash, I knew where I had heard the words that kept rising up in my consciousness. Now, I knew!

When I used to join the line of homeless people, waiting for the soup kitchen doors to open, more than once, the man who finally opened the doors would speak to us while we ate.

"Give your life to Jesus! He invites everyone to come to Him. Listen, He says, 'Come unto Me, all you who are weary.'

"You people are all weary of life. Some are old and some young. Jesus invites you all to come to Him and be saved from your sins. From your old life!"

I used to barely pay any attention to his message. I was too hungry, too stoned, or too befuddled with drink to really listen to what he said. I wanted the food in front of me.

But now, in this dark hour, the words came back to me with a tone of love, of comfort, and of hope.

I had thought all hope was gone. My life was at the bottom. There was no place to go.

Now, this voice told me to come? Come where?

To Jesus? That seemed weird. I knew all about Jesus, I thought.

I recalled my brushes with religion in Werkendam. I could still picture how angry the elder had been when we had drunken up all the communion wine. I also remembered how the religious people had treated those girls after the war had been over. I saw their vindictive, hate-filled eyes, shouting at the girls.

But something else began probing into my memory.

Hans and Walter. Those two German soldiers, praying in my bedroom, crying. I remembered how moved I had been that these men, whom I had considered enemies, could have such depth of feeling, of faith.

I also remembered the old pastor, climbing up on the rubbish pile of the demolished church, crying out, "There is still victory in Jesus!" Those words had never left me.

"Come!" The words were tender, loving, and beseeching.

Tears began streaming down my face. I turned away from the darkness below.

"Mr. Visser, how are you today?"

I opened up my eyes enough to see who was speaking. Beside my hospital bed, I saw a pleasant-looking man addressing me.

"May I call you Tom? I came to tell you some good news. News about Jesus Christ!"

I closed my eyes again. Perhaps he would go away.

For a moment, the scene on the bridge flashed through my mind. I tried to push it away.

"You are just a young man, Tom, and Jesus can save you and make you a mighty man for him! Do you want me to tell you about Him?"

This man was persistent! I opened my eyes wearily and looked at him. On his jacket, I read Jim Evans, Chaplain.

"Look, Jim, I have a question. This Jesus you talk about, how can you prove He is alive? Thousands of years ago, He was killed by the Romans. Crucified on a cross. Prove to me that He is alive." Even though I tried to keep my voice neutral, he must have heard that I really did want to know.

"That is a good question, Tom," Jim said earnestly. "Many people ask that.

"For me, it is not difficult to know that Jesus is alive. I have experienced Him and He has saved me from sin. I know He is alive because of the power He gives me to live above sin." Then, he paused for a moment.

"For you to understand, Tom, is like trying to explain to someone how a steak tastes that has never eaten any meat. Would you say it tastes sweet, sour, or salty?" There was a gentle smile on his face.

"I'd say it tastes good," I grunted. "Although it has been a while since I tasted one."

"For me to prove to you that Jesus is alive is the same way. So, I tell you, try it! You ask Jesus to reveal Himself to you! Prove Himself!"

I was having a difficult time following the conversation. My drug-riddled body was weak and I had barely enough strength to speak.

"Come to our services on Main Street in downtown. You can hear more about Jesus!" Jim must have seen how addled my brain was.

I moaned as I was hit with another spasm.

Someone must have found me, spaced out beside some city street and brought me here to the hospital. I had no memory of it.

Even though I had not thrown myself over the edge of the bridge, the very next day, I had begged a hit from a druggie and oblivious to anything, had fallen into a stupor. Now, here I was, rescued once more from the jaws of death and wondering why I was still alive.

"Come unto Me, and I will give you rest," the words kept running through my mind, over and over again. I turned restlessly on my bed.

Was it the word, "Come!" that finally made me go downtown and find the address Jim had given me? Was it the emptiness that yawned deep inside of my very being?

The door was slightly ajar, and I could hear music spilling out onto the sidewalk. I stood still for a moment, trying to decide whether I really wanted to go inside.

Once more, I could see the twisted faces of the crowd in Werkendam, shouting at the girls. "Sinners!"

Without a doubt, I knew I was a sinner. Would I be welcome here? Was there any place for sinners in a church?

There I stood, in indecision. This was not characteristic of me at all. I was usually not afraid of anything, anyone. First to enter into a fray, begin a new venture, or do something just to try it out, my nature was bold and outgoing. Why was I now finding it difficult to enter this building?

Was I afraid? Afraid of what?

A lady stepped up, and pushed the door open. I followed her.

"Welcome, brother!" A rotund man came towards me, beaming. "Welcome to the house of God!"

"I am not your brother!" The smart remark flew out of my

mouth.

He hesitated a moment, and then several more men came and shook my hand. "Welcome, welcome!"

I was overwhelmed. This was so unusual! Normally, it was I who made the moves, I who was in control. Well, not lately, for I had turned into a street bum. But now, here were these people, all being friendly and calling me brother!

The air seemed stifling. More people kept coming in the door and suddenly, I wanted to get out.

"My name is Lamar. Come! I will show you where to sit!" A young man came up to me.

"I need to smoke. I'll, I'll be right back!" I turned and pushed through the crowd.

Frantically, I looked at the knot of people in front of a bus stop. I joined the line.

I did not care where the bus would take me. I had to get away! My heart was pounding.

I was boarding the bus, when I heard a voice behind me, "Wait! Don't leave!"

I looked over my shoulder. It was Lamar.

"Where are you going?" He grabbed my shoulder.

"I was just looking inside," I managed to say.

"No! No! Come with me! The service is about to start," Lamar was persistent and steered me away from the bus.

"Look, young man," I said looking at Lamar, "I will come to your service, but I am going to make a deal with you. Your bunch says that Jesus is real and alive. That is what you say.

"Here's the deal. If your God is so real as you say He is, then I want a sign. I remember hearing from some of those Salvation Army guys these words, 'Come unto Me, all you who are weary and heavy laden and I will give you rest.'

"If your minister uses those words tonight - without you telling him about this deal- then I will believe in your God, your Jesus."

Lamar at first looked quizzically at me, then said, "I don't know. I just got here and I think we have a guest speaker. I am sure he already has his sermon all picked out."

I shrugged my shoulders, "I don't care. That's the deal."

"Come on," Lamar said briskly, "I will accept the challenge."

I followed him inside, thinking I would fix this religious bunch. I even followed Lamar all the way to the front of the meeting hall, not looking at the bulletin someone shoved into my hand.

The crowd was singing, some lifting their hands and praising God. The congregation seemed noisy to me, not at all what I had expected in a church. In Holland, the services had always been very orderly, and no one had dared breach the customs.

Then, I looked at the paper in my hands.

"COME UNTO ME ALL YE THAT ARE WEARY AND HEAVY LADEN, AND I WILL GIVE YOU REST!" The words leaped off the page at me!

I felt my chest heave! A feeling of wonder seized me! I read the words again!

The very words were used that I had bargained with Lamar! Or, had I really been bargaining with God?

I began to realize I was no longer in control. Something, I did not know what, was much greater than I could begin to comprehend.

"Guest speaker: Jack West." It was not even the regular speaker. Someone from somewhere else.

How could it be possible? How could a man from some other place know about my deal, my bargain? Even no one here knew about it, except Lamar! What was happening?

"If your minister uses those words tonight, then I will believe in your God, your Jesus!" My words came at me with startling clarity.

"You are real!" That may have been my first real prayer. I was in awe.

"I want to tell you about some of the most powerful words that were ever written," Mr. West started right in. "These words were spoken by Jesus Christ, the son of God. These words were spoken for the people back in history, and more important for us, they are spoken to us today!" His dark eyes looked directly at me.

"Jesus invites all the people, all over the world, to come to Him! Let me tell you about this amazing man!"

I sat spellbound, listening to every word.

"Are you weary?" Mr. West asked frankly after talking for over half an hour. His eyes traveled over the room, and whenever I looked up, he seemed to rest his eyes on me.

"If you feel the Holy Spirit calling you, listen to His voice. It is the voice of Jesus, saying, 'Come!'."

There it was again! That word, "Come!" The same word I had heard on the bridge. The word that never seemed to leave my head anymore.

"If the pastor uses the words, 'Come unto me, all ye that are weary and heavy laden,' I will believe in God." I really had said those words.

Once more, Mr. West asked, "Are you weary? If so, come! Come and kneel down before God and ask Jesus to come into your heart and to forgive the sins you have done.

"We all have sinned. We all need forgiveness of our sins. The blood of Jesus was shed so we can have forgiveness and rest for our weary soul."

I was on my feet, tears streaming down my face, as I almost rushed the few feet to the front. I knelt on the floor, right by the raised platform and I felt a powerful surge go through me.

"I'm sorry!" The first words that came to me sprang out of my mouth. "I'm sorry for all the wrong things I have done. For the times I cheated people, the times I lied in order to gain advantage over others.

"I'm sorry for doing drugs and for getting drunk. I'm sorry for my empty promises to Tina and the children. I'm sorry for..." There were so many things to repent from. Like a series of printed pictures, the scenes flipped through my mind.

For each one, I repented. I asked God to forgive me in the

name of Jesus.

"I will come," I finally gasped, my chest all hollow from weeping. "I believe in You, Jesus Christ. I know you are God."

I felt something stirring deep inside of me. A great welling of emotion swept over me.

"Thank You, Jesus! Oh, thank You for what You are doing for me! Thank You for Your mercy in loving me while I was still such a sinner!" Beside me, I heard Mr. West praying along with me. I heard his words of thanks.

There must have been others there, praying, but it was as though I was in a world all my own. My heart had broken before God and He was reaching down from heaven, or where ever He is and listening to my cry. I was sure of that!

Time stopped for me. There were so many emotions flooding my memory, my heart.

"Now I see how in Your love, you kept me alive, even while I was a young boy. You saved me from the German soldier's bullet and you picked me and my sister up and put us into the ditch when the mortars exploded all around us.

"In my rebellion, you watched over me. You allowed me to drink the wine of success, only to find out that riches and money were not satisfactory. You gave me Tina and the children, only to show me if I was not the man You wanted me to be, I lost them, too. Bring them back, oh, Lord!"

On and on I prayed. "Now I know what Hans and Walter were doing in my bedroom in Werkendam. They were talking to You! Oh, Lord, wherever they are, can you tell them that the little boy who saw them is now your son, too? Can you tell them that I will one day tell them how much that meant to me?

"That old pastor who planted the flag on the rubble, is he there, too? He was old then, so I think he is there with You. Tell him that one little boy who saw his faith, remembers the words, 'There is victory in Jesus!' Now I know what he meant!"

My heart was so full of thanks for what God had taken me through so I could experience His love in my heart. I realized that I must have been saved for a reason.

"I will serve You! I will live for You! I give my life into Your hands!"

CHAPTER NINE

START OVER

"Where are you?" Tina's voice came over the telephone.

"I am in a place called Brockville. It's just a small town, Tina, but I had to get away from the city. I tell you, I have started a new life." How I longed that Tina would understand.

"New life, Tom. I have heard that one before." I could hear the skepticism dripping from her voice.

"I tell you, dear, my life has changed completely! I am saved!"

There was a silence.

"Tina? Are you there?"

"Yes, Tom, I am here. What are you saved from?"

I felt tears prick my eyelids. I knew that I was not making sense to her. "Tina, I am saved from being a sinner! I believe in Jesus Christ! He has forgiven my sins and I am a new person! I stopped sinning!"

"If you think I will believe you are now perfect, Tom Visser, you have another guess coming! I know you too well!" This time, her voice mirrored the anger and hurt she carried in her heart toward me.

"I am so sorry," I could barely speak for my tears. "You have every right to distrust me, Tina. All I ask is that you come. Bring the children and you will have to see the difference in me." I did not know how else to explain to my wife what had happened, what was happening.

After a while, Tina asked, "Where are you living?"

"Uh, right now, I am staying in a motel. But I want to rent a house for us!"

"A motel? How can you afford to stay in a motel? I thought you were broke? Do you have a job?"

I tried to talk fast, as I had used to do. "Listen, the most fabulous thing happened..." my voice trailed off as I realized what I was doing. Fabricating tales had been such a part of my life! The Spirit was convicting me of starting in again.

"Well," I started off once more in a calm voice, "when I came to Brockville, I met this man, named Klaus, in a restaurant. I began talking to him, and you see, what Jesus has done for me has made such a difference in my life, I immediately began telling him about my experience.

"He said he did not understand, but thought something wonderful must have happened, and then, he invited me to stay in his motel until I could get a job and rent a house! I know this all happened because God is looking out after me!" My voice trembled as I tried to tell my wife what had happened.

"Klaus? That sounds like a German man to me. I thought you hated all Germans!"

"At first, when I realized he was German, I wanted to leave, but something has happened inside of me. I no longer hate Germans! God has given me a love even for them!"

Once more I begged, "Tina, will you come? Will you bring the children and come? I really still love you and the children. I want to be a good husband to you and a good daddy to the children. Please come."

"Oh, I am sure this will do, Mr. Chesney!" I looked around inside the little house. "What do you think, Tina?"

My wife looked into the small kitchen. I sensed her hesitation, but I was quiet. I had decided I would not force her to move if she didn't like it.

At first, when Tina had stepped off the bus in Brockville, holding our baby son, Jerritt and our six year old daughter behind her, it had seemed too good to be true. A few days of living in the motel had convinced me to quickly seek a house to rent.

Mr. Chesney waited on our response. "I know it is small, but it is close to town and should not be difficult to heat in the winter. It is yours if you want it."

Want it? I could hardly contain myself. I had hardly known how to pray, I knew I had desperately been asking God to find a house for us. I was sure He had.

"It will be all right," Tina said, smiling a sad, little smile.

My heart smote me. I knew what she was thinking. She did not think it would last.

"Then, you can move right in," Mr. Chesney said. "You are welcome to use the furniture and dishes and whatever else is in here. The last renters just moved out and left everything. Including a mess."

"Don't worry, we will clean it!" It was hard to keep the joy out of my voice.

"I just thank God we found something! Thank you very much, Mr. Chesney!"

"Call me Frank," the elderly man smiled. "I am glad to have found a Christian couple to live in here. You can pray in this house all you want!"

I looked quickly at Tina, and then turning to Frank, I said, "God has truly answered my prayers. I am only a new Christian and there are so many more things I need to learn. Thank you for encouraging me to pray in this house. I will!"

"Welcome to God's kingdom," Frank reached out and shook my hand.

"Tina, I want you to know the peace of Christ like I know it," The children were in bed and Tina and I were spending our first evening together, talking.

"All the things that you have taken me through, Tom, and now this? Why can't we just live like normal people? All the time I was back with my parents, I kept wondering what I have done to deserve just a life like this. Sure, I have not always lived right, but should I be punished more than anyone else? Tom, you know you have put us through an awful life. You spent money on drugs and drink until our entire life was gone. Now, you want me to believe like you do! I just can't." Tina's face showed the strain she was going through.

"I will pray for you that you understand," I said. "I know everything you said is true, but I am different," I insisted.

"Then prove it," she said curtly. "I am going to bed."

I found myself sitting in the living room a long time that evening. I began telling God everything.

"You know, God, what you have done in my life. You know I am different. How can I make Tina see it?

"I want to raise my children to love you. They will not if my wife does not believe. Please, make her believe."

In the darkness of that room, I heard a soft voice speak to me. "Tom, how long did it take you to come to Me? How long did you fight against Me before you understood?"

It was true. I had to come to the end of my self-sufficiency before I had cried out to God.

The walk home from town was not far, but this evening, I wished it had been further. I had been looking for work, but there seemed to be no jobs. "No, sir, not hiring." Over and over again I heard the same words.

I opened the front door and stepped inside. It was already late and I saw Tina sitting at the kitchen table, her head propped up in her hands.

"What is there to eat?" I asked, trying to sound cheerful.

"Nothing," her voice was muffled. She did not bother raising her head from her hands.

It was quiet in our little house. Anita and the baby must have already been put to bed.

"What did the children eat?"

"I gave them the last pieces of bread. Did you get a job today?"

I bowed my head and in a low voice, said, "No."

"We'll have to go back to my mother," Tina said in a monotone. "This is not working. We cannot feed the children, there is no money to buy anything. Our life is no different!"

In the middle of my despondency, a thought came to me. "Pray."

For only a moment, I hesitated. Then, I walked over to my wife and pulled her up from her chair. "Come, pray with me."

"It won't do any good," she said, although she followed me to our small living room.

"God," I prayed as we knelt beside the sofa, "I bring our need to You. You see how desperate we are. Our children are hungry. I cannot find a job. Will You tell us what to do?"

In the darkness, we waited.

When I first heard a step on the front porch, I did not even let it sink into my consciousness. I was praying. Desperately praying.

"Hello! Tom! Tina!"

"It's Frank!" I quickly stood up and went toward the front door. "Whatever does he want this evening?"

"Tom! How are you?" Frank cheerfully greeted me. "Oh! Hi Tina! You folks not in bed yet, are you?"

"Come in!" I pushed the door open.

Carrying a cardboard box, Frank entered and put the box into my arms.

"Here! I stopped at the bread store this evening, and I thought about your little family. I knew you are still getting on your feet, so I thought I would bring it right over this evening?"

I looked in amazement at the loaves of bread in the box. Cellophane wrapped cakes were on one side.

"Have you found a job yet? No? Well, I am sure God will provide something. There is some new construction going on the other side of town. A new strip mall or something. Maybe those guys are hiring."

"You are an angel, Frank," I said gratefully, putting the box on the kitchen table. "Look, Tina, what God has sent us! Right as we were praying!"

"Oh, I don't think I make a very good angel," Frank laughed, backing out the door. "I haven't the beginning of any wings. Good night!"

"Let's get Anita up and give her some cake," I looked eagerly at Tina. "I want to tell her how God answered our prayers!"

Tina smiled at my joy. "All right. But I think you better tell her Frank brought the food, not God."

Even though she said that, as we gathered around the table and ate cake, I could tell that Tina was in deep thought. I thanked God over and over for hearing my prayer.

"Rick, check this out!" I called to my new friend. "The building is almost completed, except for the cleaning up from the construction dirt. Let's see if we can get a job here." I   had met Rick in Brockville. Like me, he was a new Christian, and like me, he was out of work.

The plaza on the outskirts of town was huge and I was eager to see if we could find employment here.

"I know. I have been here before to see the manager about getting a job," Rick did not seem very confident.

"Doesn't hurt to ask," I said, as we rounded the corner.

The little scene in front of us stopped us in our tracks.

"I don't care what you say!" A man in a hard hat was yelling at two young men. "This was to be done two days ago, and here I come, expecting to have the place cleaned out, and I find crap all over the place!" Then, he spewed out a string of profanity, including using the name of my Savior as a swear word.

"Sir!" The word leaped out of my mouth as I stepped toward him. "I rebuke you to use the name of Jesus like that! God tells us we are not to swear! I know you are angry, but do not use the name of our holy God in anger!"

The tall man stared at me, then burst out with, "Wou in the world are you? What do you want? Are you the preacher of this plaza?"

I smiled at him. "No, I am not a preacher. Actually, I am looking for a job. Do you know of someone who could use a worker? Perhaps a janitor or someone to clean up after the construction workers have left?"

But he had already turned and jumping into his pick up truck, gunned the engine and left.

"That was the boss," one of the young men said, grinning at me. "I don't think he will want you working for him. If you think he was angry today, you should hear him when he really gets going!"

"I guess you blew that job prospect," Rick told me as we left, heading for town. "Better look somewhere else for work."

"There is no chance," Rick protested a week later as we once more made the rounds, looking for work. "That boss man will still recognize you. You want to see if he has stopped swearing, or what?"

"I just know I need work. My landlord has helped us so often with food and my wife is about ready to go back to her mother. I have to find work!" My faith was being sorely tried.

"Here goes nothing," Rick said in a resigned tone as we headed out for the plaza.

We had just stepped inside the door when I heard a man's voice yelling, "Hey! You! Preacher! Apostle Paul!"

I looked around. It was the boss man!

"Come here! I want to talk to you."

He seemed to be in a better mood this time. "I remember you. You are the one that talked to me about swearing." He looked quizzically at me. "What made you talk to me that day?"

"Because I am a Christian," I said simply. "It hurts me to hear anyone use the name of Jesus as a swear word, when He means so much to me."

The man looked at the floor. "I know I shouldn't swear. I know it is wrong.

"All day long, your rebuke stayed with me. I know about those things, you see, for I had a Godly grandmother. She raised me and tried to get me to go to church with her. She was a wonderful woman. But I have not thought about her or my childhood for a long time."

Looking up at me, he put out his hand. "I am Mr. Turner. Is there anything I can do for you?"

"My name is Tom and this is my friend, Rick. We are interested in applying for a janitorial position here in the plaza."

"Experienced?"

"Yes, sir. I had a cleaning business in Halifax. We did mostly windows, but we did some other cleaning, too."

"Come with me to my office."

"You can pray anywhere," the pastor had told us.

It had been good to find a small fellowship that encouraged me in my new faith in Christ. I hardly knew anyone there, but I was blessed by the teachings.

Now, on my way home from work, I was suddenly smitten by those words. My heart was heavy, and I was beginning to wonder if Tina would ever become a Christian. For weeks now, I had been praying.

"Look! God has been so good to us! I have a job, and we have this little house! My life has changed and we are deeply blessed! Tina, what can I do to help you see that you need Jesus?" Over and over again, I had tried to convince my wife.

"Don't waste your time praying for me," she would tell me over and over again. "I'm glad it works for you, but for me...."

The gravel crunched underneath my feet as I walked beside the road. "Pray anywhere."

It was a lonely stretch of road, but I did not care if anyone saw me or not. I knelt beside the road on the berm and began to pray. I did not have words, but my heart was so heavy for my wife and I began to plead with God to speak to my wife.

"I know I have not been a good testimony, but God speak to her in spite of me! Help her to know You! Talk to her! I don't know what to say to this woman anymore. I give her to You!"

"Tina! I'm home!" I glanced into the kitchen. "Where are you?"

There was no answer. I walked into the living room. "Tina!" I gasped.

"Oh, Tom!" Her voice reached me from the floor where she was sitting. "Look! I understand!"

Her voice was choked with tears, yet she lifted a smiling face toward me. "I understand! I believe in Jesus!"

I was down on the floor beside her, weeping with joy! I was filled with wonder at what was happening to my wife!

"All afternoon, I kept thinking about life and the meaning of life. I knew that God had done something wonderful in your heart, and even though I wanted it too, I did not want to let go. I don't know if it makes sense or not, but something kept me back!" Her words tumbled out.

"Look, here in this song book! This is how I feel!" Her finger pointed to an open song book on the floor in front of her.

"All to Jesus, I surrender! All to Him I freely give. I surrender all! I surrender all!" I read the words out loud.

"All to Jesus, I surrender! I surrender all!" Her voice, shaking with emotion, joined me in reading the wonderful words.

What a day of rejoicing! We wept and laughed together in her newfound joy.

"Now I understand," she kept saying to me, as I hugged her over and over again. "Now, your Jesus is my Jesus!"

CHAPTER TEN

POWER!

"There are many people looking for something fulfilling, something meaningful to make life worth living!" I spoke loudly into the microphone I held close to my mouth. "I want to tell you how to get high on LSD!"

A cheer went up from the group of long haired hippies sitting on the grass in the middle of the square in Hamilton, Ontario. This was the 60's, and our town, as well as the towns and cities all over North America, had its share of young people, disillusioned with life, living in communes and living together in run down houses or drifting from place to place, camping and living in their vehicles.

"We all want some experience that makes us feel good. For many, that only lasts for several days, but I will tell you about a high that lasts for much longer!"

"Tell us!"

"Way to rock, man!"

I smiled at them and even as I began to speak again, I noticed more and more people, attracted by the crowd gathered around me, coming to see what was happening.

"You say you want peace. No more fighting or wars. Get out of Vietnam, America, you say!"

Another loud cheer went up. One young man, dressed in a long robe, unwound his bandana from his head and began waving it back and forth, chanting, "Peace! Karma! Peace! Karma!" The seated group swayed back and forth, rocking on their haunches.

More and more passersby stopped, and then curiously worked their way closer. Young people from the town joined the crowd. They seemed glad for a diversion from the usual quiet Sunday afternoons in town.

"You know, when I take drugs, I get that immediate rush that all druggies crave. The excitement, the feeling of power, of love and the spaced out feeling rushes in and nothing on earth seems to matter." I looked directly at the hippies. "But those times always end, and it seems like every time afterwards, I have to take more in order to get the same lift, the same excitement!"

"Yeah! That stinks," one young woman, her long hair

flowing down over her shoulders agreed. "Always need more the next time."

"Sister," I addressed her, "I see you have experienced what that does to your body." Her sunken eyes and mottled skin stretched over her cheekbones were all too familiar.

"Let me tell you something much better," I began to speak into the microphone again, stepping back and trailing the cord from the loud speaker behind me. "I want...."

"Sir!" A loud voice interrupted me. I looked to my left and saw two policemen approaching me.

"Yes?" I addressed them politely.

"We have received a complaint that you are disturbing the peace," the one officer told me. "You have to stop your meeting."

A chorus of jeers went up from the hippies.

"Let him alone!"

"Police harassment!"

The policeman looked quickly at the restive crowd and then said in a low tone, "See, we may have to take you into custody to protect you from them. They could become violent!"

Shaking my head, I said, "But I am not afraid. They are listening to what I am telling them! They want to hear!"

"But you don't have written permission from the police station! This meeting must disperse!" I could hear the note of authority in the speaker's voice.

I chuckled. "But I do have permission! I asked the chief of police, Officer Schmitt to conduct this meeting!"

The two policemen glanced at each other. "We don't know about this."

"Call him and ask him! Tell him that Tom Visser is having a meeting on the town square, just as he gave me permission to do!"

The radio crackled and I could hear Mr. Schmitt's voice. "What? Tom Visser? Oh, yes! He is? I did not think he was serious."

"Look," I said, "Please allow me to continue! I have his permission."

They were quiet, but the crowd wasn't. "Let the man speak!"

"Anyway, I am not in control here," I told them.

"Then who is?" One of the policeman asked quickly.

I leaned close to him. "Jesus Christ!" Then, I lifted the microphone to my mouth again, and continued to speak.

I noticed the policemen backed off, but they did not leave. I did not care. I rested in the assurance that I had the highest authority I needed to speak.

"The LSD I want to talk to you today is something that is much greater and longer lasting than anything you have ever experienced before!

"The L is love!"

"Yeah!" Several of the people threw their arms around each other, and grinned at me.

Then I began speaking about my life, simply telling them my testimony. I told them about my childhood in Holland, my immigration to Canada and my success as a businessman.

The crowd grew very quiet as I told them about my experience on the Jacque Cartier Bridge. One young woman had tears streaming down her face.

"The S is for salvation!" I told them about my experience in church, and how I had felt the love of Jesus come into my life. "I was saved! I am saved!"

I closed with the last letter. "The D is for deliverance! There is deliverance for everyone who repents and believes in Jesus Christ!" I appealed to them to honestly look at their lives and see if they liked what they saw there. I gripped the microphone tightly and looked out over the crowd. To my amazement, there must have been over two hundred people gathered around.

I was truly thankful for the loud speaker system. I knew everyone could hear clearly.

It had not been easy to find a speaker system. When the seed of my idea had first been planted in my mind by the Holy Spirit, I had immediately gone to the churches and asked to use their systems.

"We have to meet with the board and get their approval."

"Street ministry? If the people want to hear about God, they can come to church. We have many churches in Hamilton."

"Our pastor is on his holiday. Wait until he comes back."

Time and again, I had been turned down. It had been then that I had gone to the coven and asked them. That's right, the devil worshippers.

"You want to do what?" The lanky man asked me, his breath fragrant with his most recent "hit".

Then, he had laughingly agreed. "Take it, brother. See what will happen."

So, here I was, using the first speaker system I had been able to borrow. It had been then that I had placed a big ad in the local newspaper, inviting everyone to come and hear how to get high on LSD. I had extended a special welcome to all the hippies, the homeless, and the people looking for meaning in their lives.

"I want you to be honest," I told the crowd. "If you have never experienced the love and salvation and deliverance that Jesus can give you, to ask Him sincerely if He is real! Meet Him squarely and tell Jesus that you want an 'out' from your life of frustration and meaninglessness! While I pray, if you want to repent from your sins, you come right up here and kneel on the grass and ask Jesus Christ, the son of God to make you clean! You ask Him for His forgiveness and to fill your heart with His Spirit!"

"One of the first ways to show God that you mean business is to get rid of all your drugs! Those drugs do not last, as you well know. They make you weak and dependant and do just the opposite from what you really want in your life. Get rid of them! Bring them to Jesus!

"This is the beginning of the offering you can make! Bring them up here and we will make a pile! This pile will be destroyed to show all the people that you mean business!"

I began to pray.

The Spirit began to move among the people. I heard people weeping, and there were was a stir as first, several, and then more and more people came forward, weeping and kneeling down on the grass. Drug paraphernalia began to pile up in front of me.

"Hallelujah to the most High, Jesus Christ, the Son of God!" Words of praise leaped from my mouth.

"Tell Jesus all about your sins! Tell Him you are sorry for the wrongs you have done!" I knelt with them and continued to pray. I began stuffing the drugs into my pockets. I did not want any unscrupulous ones to have opportunity to get free drugs!

I give all glory to God for what He did that day. More than thirty people were gathered together, weeping and praying. Together, we cried out to Jesus to have mercy on us, to save us! I know the prayers were the sweet incense that our heavenly Father is longing to hear. My heart was filled to overflowing as I saw the people cry out to Him for mercy.

I was blessed to see that one of the policemen was wiping away tears from his eyes. Now, he truly knew that I was not in control of the meeting, but Jesus Christ was!

The next day, a member from the Royal Mounted policemen came to me and said, "Mr. Visser, I am here to confiscate the drugs that you took away yesterday. I want a list of the names of the people who had those drugs."

I rejoiced that the news of the previous day was spreading through our town. "Sir, I have flushed all the drugs down the toilet and as for the names, I do not have a list of them. Many of those people I had not met before and if God forgave them, then surely we can do the same."

Then, a glorious thought struck me. "You know, sir, there is a list of the names of those that repented and believe in Jesus! You see, in heaven there is a list recording all those that have joined the family of God! Yes, Glory to Jesus, there is a list! A list of those that are saved! The angels are rejoicing over the lost sinners that have repented!"

Dimly, through the fog of sleep, I heard the telephone ring.

"Tom, the telephone is ringing," Tina was pushing my shoulder.

I stumbled out to the living room in the dark and found the phone.

"Hello!"

"It's Jon-Jon, Mr. Visser. Do you remember me?"

I tried to sort through the maze of my acquaintances.

"You know, from the coven! You used our speaker system for your meeting in the park!" Ahh! Now I remembered. "Yes, Jon-Jon, now I remember you."

"Listen. You say your God is all powerful, right? Well, I have a situation here that will prove it.

"One of our girls, Shelay, was hypnotized and she does not come out of her hypnosis. We want to know if your God is strong enough to bring her out."

Now I was fully awake. "You say she doesn't come out of her trance? How long has she been out?"

"I don't know. We don't keep track of time. Just a long time. But we can pinch her, stick pins in her and there is no response." Even though he tried to keep his voice neutral, I could hear a note of worry coming over the line.

"There is no question if my God is powerful enough, Jon-Jon," I told him firmly. "I will come."

"Tina, pray!" I told my wife the situation as I hurriedly dressed. "The demons and devils are trying to get complete control of this girl."

"Don't go by yourself," Tina grabbed my arm. "Take someone with you!"

Ahh, yes! "I will call Dr. Gouther! He has been teaching on how we should meet the needs of the people with the message of the Gospel." It took some time to rouse my teacher from the Bible School where I was taking classes.

"Tom! You want me to do what?"

"Listen, Dr. Gouther, I have no time to explain any more. I will be at your house in ten minutes to pick you up!"

I went out into the chilly night and jumped into our car. I glanced at my wristwatch as I opened the car door. 2:30.

When no one came to the door at Dr. Gouther's house, I turned the car off and ran up the walk and knocked.

"Tom, I am not sure if this is wise," Dr. Gouther said as soon as he opened the door. "The people at the coven are demon-filled!"

"Come on," I grabbed him and pulled him out the door and down the sidewalk.

I started the engine, and immediately, the windshield clouded up.

"Look!" Dr. Gouther said, pointing to the windshield, his voice quavering, "The window is fogging up! This might be a sign from God that He does not want us to go!"

I heard the fear in his voice.

"Dear God," I prayed. "I know that You are all powerful. I claim the power over this situation in the name of Jesus! His blood has covered my sins and the sins of all those that truly believe in You! We will only go in the power of Your Son, Jesus Christ!"

Beside me, I could hear Dr. Gouther praying.

"Look, the window is clear!" I said exultantly after our prayer. "God is with us!"

Jon-Jon was at the door of their building as we parked the car. "This way," he said and we followed him down a dark hall and then into a dim, musky-smelling room.

It was all too familiar for me. How often I had been a part of such a drug den, huddled together with pot heads, feeling the oppression of evil spirits.

"There she is," Jon-Jon said dully, pointing to the floor.

A surge of anger, then of pity, went through my being. Anger against Satan, anger against the Christians who had not effectively counterattacked this great evil that was claiming the lives of many of these poor children. For children they were, deep in the grip of Satan.

Pity for the girl, lying white and still on a dirty blanket, her eyes open and staring into space. I could barely see her in the dim light, but there was something that looked vaguely familiar.

Turning to address the group in the room, I said, "Out! All

of you! There are already too many demons in this room! I command you all to leave in the name of Jesus Christ, the Holy One of God!"

There was an immediate shuffle of feet as the group began to disperse.

"I must stay," Jon-Jon told me. "If Shelay comes out of her coma, she will be frightened if she does not see anyone she recognizes. It is important for those coming out of the trance to be in the same situation as they were when they left their bodies."

I stepped closer for a better look at the girl he called Shelay. Then, triumphantly, I turned to Jon-Jon.

"That is not Shelay! I know her! This is Amy!"

Jon-Jon stepped back, his eyes darting over my face. How, how did you know?"

"I met her in Hamilton at a street meeting. There was this girl that kept mocking me while I told people about Jesus Christ and I asked her name. I told her, 'Amy, there will come a time when you will be in deep trouble and you will need God.'

"This is the same young woman! Now, go out with all of your sorceries and witchcraft!" I pushed him out into the hall and closed the door.

Dr. Gouther and I knelt beside the still figure of Amy. We began to pray.

"In the all powerful name of Jesus Christ, the Son of the most high God, I rebuke Satan, the evil one. By the blood of Jesus Christ, who has been given to cleanse us from all of our sins, I renounce the power of Satan over this girl, who belongs to God."

I felt the power of the Holy Spirit surge through me. I prayed again and I was not amazed to see tears began to stream from Amy's eyes. Then, she opened her eyes and looked straight at me.

"It's you!" she managed to whisper.

"Yes," I told her gently, but firmly. "I told you there would come a time when you needed God. The time has come."

We helped her sit up. Then, she bowed her head and began sobbing loudly. "I have sinned! Oh, I have sinned against God! Is there any hope left for me?"

It was obvious that she had been taught about God. "I turned away from Him! I did not listen to my parents and left the church. Oh, is there any hope?"

As tenderly as I could, I began telling Amy about the mercifulness and love of our Savior. I spoke of her sins and her need for repentance.

"I want to repent! Oh, I am so sorry for ever joining Satan's group. It is so scary! Help! Oh, help!"

Victory was not easy as Satan and his demons fought to keep her under their power.

But, glory hallelujah! The power of Jesus Christ was much stronger, and as the wretched cries for help continued to ring out in that den, the healing power of Christ came in gentle, loving arms and wrapped around the rescued girl.

I became aware of shadowy figures coming into the room as Amy's voice reached into the rest of the rooms of the house.

I began to pray for all of them. "Father in heaven, You said in your word, 'Let the children come unto me'. You never said which children. I am here to bring these lost children to You. Please, Lord, they have no daddy. Please, you be their daddy. I claim these children for you today."

We moved away from Hamilton shortly after this, and later, I had the opportunity to return and preach in a meeting house. After the meeting, there was a commotion and people were yelling, "Tom! Tom!" and waving handkerchiefs.

"It's us! Don't you remember?"

I could hardly believe my eyes. It was Amy and a number of her friends. "We are saved! We love Jesus and have been baptized!"

God had reached down into the coven and delivered many from the clutches of Satan. "Jon-Jon has become a follower of Jesus Christ!"

Tears streamed down my eyes as I hugged them and we praised God together.

"Now we know the Jesus you told us about! He is our Jesus, too!"

CHAPTER ELEVEN

SOWING SEEDS

"Come on, Dutch preacher, give me five dollars," Brian, a dark haired young man begged. "You got the money, I know. You just got paid for your cleaning jobs."

At first, I just looked at him, sitting at our kitchen table, nervously twiddling his fingers around his coffee mug.

"Brian, what is it?" I asked, trying to figure out what to do with this guy we had been trying to reach for months. "Just what is it that you want? Why are you continually at odds with the world?"

"Preacher man! I'm not at odds with the world! Man, I only ask for five dollars? What is so big about that?" His eyebrows dropped into a frown.

"I want to give you more than five dollars," I told him. "I want to give you Jesus."

Before I could say more, he jumped up from his chair and came around the table towards me. Tina jumped up in alarm from her seat and Anita got up and went to her mother's side. Our son, Jerrit, sat wide-eyed in his high chair.

"You want to fight?" I asked, getting up. "Come on outside, Brian! You want to fight with me?" I could feel a rush of blood sweeping up over my face.

"You can't fight, Dutch preacher!" Brian taunted, reaching out and grabbing my shirt front. "You just trust in Jesus for everything!"

With one swift move, I grabbed Brian's arm and pulled him out of the kitchen into the side yard.

"Defend yourself," I told him grimly, putting up my hands.

Brian danced around on his feet, his face grinning with glee. He punched me on my shoulder and right then, I lost any inhibitions that I had.

I must say that we fought all over the side yard, and we both were off our feet and rolling around on the grass before it was over.

Finally, I got Brian face down on the grass, holding his arms pinned behind his back. I was breathing hard and I felt my left eye swelling shut.

"Here is your suitcase, Brian," I heard Tina's voice beside me. "You are leaving this place. After all the things Tom has done for you, this is the way you treat him! I have had enough! Tom, let him up!"

I got up from the ground and Brian slowly raised himself up from the ground. He kept his eyes on the ground and without saying a word, reached for his suitcase.

I felt a wave of remorse and regret sweep over me as I watched him go out of the yard and start down the sidewalk. There was a forlorn slump to his shoulders and he no longer looked arrogant and cocky.

"Tom, come inside," Tina tugged at my arm. "Fighting outside in our yard! I know Brian has been a pain, but still, fighting!"

Meekly, I followed her inside. I felt terrible about the entire episode. "Tina, I am sorry. I lost my temper when he kept at me! I know fighting won't help any situation, but I feel even worse that we were not able to help Brian! Where did we fail him?"

Tina nodded her head. I knew she, too, felt bad.

Brian had not been the first of the string of young people that we had taken into our home. There had been many. But he was the first one that we had sent away. Some had left of their own accord, either because they were ready to get on with their lives or because they were not ready to submit themselves to Christ and what we had required of them.

"Tina, let us pray for Brian." We knelt beside the sofa and prayed. "God, I am sorry that I fought with Brian. But I am even more sorry we were not able to reach him for You. You know his drug problem. You know his drinking problems. Lord, you know all his problems.

"Don't let him rest until he comes to You! Keep bothering him and don't let him find any peace until he gives his life to Jesus!"

God had blessed our little family greatly. In 1967, little Debbie was born into our family and my cleaning business had prospered enough that we were able to take in destitute young people. In my street ministry, I met people from all walks of life and many had no place to stay.

"We don't have wall to wall carpets in our house, we have

wall to wall people," I would joke to my friends.

The girls stayed upstairs and the boys slept downstairs. Tina learned to have enough soup and bread to feed hungry mouths whenever I left to evangelize on the streets. She never knew how many people I would bring home.

"It is all because of Jesus," I told them in answer to their questions.

"I don't understand," more than one would reply. "What does Jesus have to do with you inviting us to your house?"

Opening my arms, I would say, "I want to love you the way Jesus loves us. You may never have experienced true love in your life. I want to show you how much Jesus loves you."

More than once, we were able to lead some seeking, hungry soul to Jesus. Drug addicts, drunkards, prostitutes; they all were welcome. This was my ministry, my calling.

"Tina! Wake up!" I shook my wife's shoulder gently.

Sitting upright in the bed, she looked at me. "Why are you dressed? Is it morning?" She looked at the clock. "It's only one o'clock!"

"I know, dear. I had a dream. I am to go to town. Someone is in need. I need to go." Even to my ears, it didn't make sense.

"You are going to town because of a dream? Why can't it wait?"

"Tina, you pray for me. I don't know, but there is something urgent that spoke to me. I think it is the voice of God. Someone was trying to commit suicide or something."

My faithful truck started right up and I headed into town. "Lord, I don't know where you want me to go, but I want you to guide my steering wheel and tell me where to go."

After making several right hand turns, I was nearing the river. The bridge loomed up ahead of me.

The dark figure of a young man suddenly loomed up right in front of me. I slammed on the brakes, and skidded sideways up onto the side walk. As the truck jerked to a stop, I cut off the ignition and jumped out.

"What is wrong? What are you trying to do?" My heart was still pounding furiously at the near miss.

The young man looked up at me with dull eyes. Then, he dropped his head and began to cry.

"Lord, is this the one?" I asked silently.

"Come into my truck," I opened the passenger door and pushed the youth inside.

"Tell me your name." I said when I had gotten in on the driver's side. "Is there anything I can do to help you?"

The pathetic young man just sat in the truck, weeping, his long hair falling around his shoulders.

"Why did you rescue me?" His words were dry and harsh, sticking in his throat. "I can't even kill myself."

"Listen," I said as I placed my hand on his shoulder, "My name is Tom and I think I can help you. Let's go to the house."

Larry's story was not so unusual. Raised by drunken parents, he had in his teen life turned to alcohol, drugs and ended up living on the streets. Now, at twenty, he thought there was nothing to live for. "Life has no meaning. I have experienced everything already. Nothing satisfies. No one cares about me or what happens to me. I want to die."

I was fairly sure he was still on drugs, but I spent most of the night, talking to him, telling him about Jesus and what He does for people. Cup after cup of tea went down his throat and in the morning, I put him into bed, praying that he would still be there and sober when I returned in the evening.

I pushed the door open and walked inside. The air was hazy with cigarette smoke, loud with music, and reeking with whiskey fumes. I had my hands full of Gospel tracts and looked around to hand someone a tract. The tables were mostly empty, but in the back a crowd was gathered, their backs turned towards me.

Suddenly a voice cried out, "The Dutch preacher man is here!" A raucous laugh rang out over the music.

"Come on over here, Preacher man!" someone yelled. "Here is something for you to see! Someone for you to save!"

"Hallelujah! Something for the preacher!"

I was bewildered. I had never experienced something like this. Usually, there were some that mocked, but for the most time, I was ignored. Why this welcome? The crowd was going wild.

Then, I saw why.

In the dim light, I could see the center of their attention. A young girl was there and the she was showing off and flirting with the men. I could tell she was enjoying the men's calls and cheers. Yet, I immediately sensed, too, that she was unhappy. There was something about her that made a great wave of pity sweep over me for her.

"Lord, show me how to help this poor girl," I prayed immediately. I knew I was facing some kind of test. "Lord, show me how to handle this situation."

I tried to keep my voice mild, but I had to raise it to speak above the music. "What are you doing, girl?"

All eyes were on me. Someone turned the music off.

"Do you know that God loves you? He does not like what you are doing, but he does love you. I know this will not bring you the happiness that you are looking for. Only a peace in our hearts can bring lasting happiness."

Looking at the men, I said, "I see a girl that is trying to make money. I see someone who is to be pitied that she has sunk to this level. But it is to your shame that you are here. This is not right. Everyone needs to repent and turn to God."

Without looking at what I was selecting, I walked toward the girl and said, "Here is something for you to read. It will tell you about Jesus."

A flush swept over the face of the girl. She looked at the tract. Then, with a gasp, she looked at me. "How did you know I am German?"

I glanced at the title of the tract. It was a German tract! VAS MUS ICH TUN UM GERETTER ZU WERRDEN? (What Must I Do to be Saved?)

I smiled and said, "I did not know, but God knows. He knows everything."

All this time, the group of men were staring at us, silently watching what was happening. The girl was staring at the tract, and then, tears began sliding down her cheeks.

The men began shrinking back and someone turned the music on again.

With tears streaming down her face, the girl said in broken words, "Will you pray for me?"

"Yes, I will gladly pray with you. But we need to get out of here. This is not a place for you. Or I.

"Repent from your sins and turn to Jesus. Turn away from your wicked ways, and Jesus will cleanse you and make you new!"

We were able to find a quiet spot out on the street bench and I spent a long time with Greta that evening, praying. I felt the presence of the Holy Spirit, guiding me to witness to that wayward woman.

"I do want Jesus to be my God," she told me before I left. "I do know that I need Him more than anything else in my life."

"I am so happy," Larry looked at me with smiling eyes. "Nothing better has ever happened to me in my life!"

He and I were having a midnight snack. All evening, I had spent with him, telling him of the saving power of Jesus Christ.

Larry had been with us for over a month. At first, it had been very difficult, for his lack of training and self-discipline had been hard for us to cope with.

But Tina and I had loved him, discipled him, and tried to be patient. Finally, that night he had said, "Tom, I want to know more about Jesus."

Now, here we were, having our midnight snack on a Sunday evening.

"I am so happy!" Larry said again. "I just love everyone, especially Jesus!" Then looking at me with his dark eyes, he said, "May I call you, Dad? I am so glad I have met you! It was you that came that night I tried to kill myself. It was your dream that made you getup in the night and look for me."

I grabbed him and gave him a big hug. "Yes, you may call me

Dad! I am proud to call you, son! It was God who brought us together."

"Is it all right if I pray before we eat?" Larry said somewhat hesitantly. "Now I know why you always pray before we eat. I feel so thankful for all God has done for me."

His prayer was very simple and straightforward. No fancy words, no repeated phrases. I could tell he was speaking straight from his heart.

Lifting shining eyes to me, he said, "Tomorrow, I am going to Hamilton to look for work. I want to make something of my life! No more sponging off other people!"

"It is strange we have not heard from Larry," I said to Tina, two evenings later.

"Perhaps he has found a job already," Tina said, wiping Jerrit's chin as we finished our supper.

"Come to Papa, Debbie!" I lifted our baby daughter and tossed her into the air. She giggled with glee.

"Someone is here!" Anita announced, looking out the window. "It's the police!"

We all got up from our chairs immediately. "I wonder if Larry is in trouble!" I could not help but be concerned. Had he been swept back into his old life?

"Are you Mr. Tom Visser?" The uniformed officer asked when I answered his knock.

"Yes, sir."

"Do you know a Larry Dissong?"

"Yes."

The officer looked at a card in his hand. "This card was found in Larry's pocket." He handed it to me.

It was a card that I gave to people whenever I talked to them about Jesus. It had my name, address, telephone number and the simple message, 'Jesus Loves You' written on it. This card was wrinkled and smudged.

"There has been an accident," the officer spoke

sympathetically. "Larry has been killed!"

I heard Tina gasp behind me. Tears squeezed out of my eyes.

"Killed?" I echoed. "What happened?"

We tried to piece the story together.

Evidently, Larry had tried to find work all day on Monday.

"Larry was hitch hiking your way when a man stopped to pick him up. It was then that they had the wreck.

The driver of the car survived and he said Larry told him he wanted to come back to your house. Just as they pulled back onto the highway, a vehicle was headed right for them, and when the driver swerved to miss him, the other vehicle smashed right into the passenger side and Larry was instantly killed."

I was sitting on a chair on our porch as the policeman told me the story. I could barely grasp what had happened.

Then, with a start, I remembered. "Oh, praise God! Oh, hallelujah!" Even though tears were streaking down my face, I lifted my hands toward heaven.

I am sure the policeman must have thought I was going crazy. Why was I praising God after this terrible accident?

"Larry is with Jesus! He had just become a Christian! Officer! Do you know what?" I was up and grabbing at the policeman's jacket. "Larry was ready to die! He accepted Jesus as his savior, just two days ago! He is in heaven!"

I turned and hugged my family. Tina's eyes were wet with tears also.

"He tried to kill himself only about a month ago, and I brought him home here and told him about Jesus! He believed only two days ago! Oh, thank You, Jesus!" I tried to explain to the officer.

"Something wonderful must have happened," the officer said as he prepared to leave. "I have never brought such sad news that brought so much joy!"

My mind went back to that dark night when Larry had tried to jump in front of my truck. "Lord, help me to always obey your voice! Thank you for saving Larry!" I shuddered to think what would have happened had I not gone out in the night, searching for him. But now, Larry was safe in heaven with Christ!

CHAPTER TWELVE

REWARDS DO COME

I boarded the airplane in the Chicago O'Hara airport in preparation for my flight back to Ontario. I was glad to get on this flight, for my first flight had been cancelled and I had had to wait several hours before this flight had become available.

Walking down the aisle, I checked for my seat number. On my boarding pass was printed clearly, 17D. Not too good a seat number, right in the middle of the center aisle.

However, I was always ready to witness to anyone I could about my faith in Jesus Christ, so I asked God to assign my seat beside someone who needed to hear the Gospel or a Christian that we could encourage each other.

When I saw my traveling companions, I thought, "Uh, oh! Not so good today!" I smiled at the Chinese man who sat in 17E and although he smiled, he did not say anything. "I might as well count him out! I don't speak Chinese, and it doesn't look as though he knows enough English to have a conversation."

Nevertheless, I had to try, so I asked him, "Do you speak English?"

A smile broke over his face and he shook his head and a stream of words, I guess they were Chinese, flowed from his mouth. I smiled at him and shook my head. Shaking heads at each other was definitely a loser here.

Then, I saw a woman stop in the aisle, glance at her boarding pass, and then at the empty seat beside me. Without a glance at me, she settled herself on the seat, fastened her seat buckle and stared straight ahead.

"One of those types," I mused to myself. Stylish, self-assured, and well, at least middle-aged, but very well preserved. Her face had a distant, non-commital look that seemed to say, "Don't bother bothering me. Please ignore me while I am ignoring you," or something of the sort.

"Hi, my name is Tom."

A frigid glance at me from her artfully made up eyes was supposed to set me in my place, I suppose, but I plunged right ahead. "Isn't this a nice day?"

I was surprised that such a sophisticated woman could deliver such a powerful snort. "Nice day! Look at the snow outside! You call this nice!" Her voice was as cold and chilly as the weather.

I was too stubborn to be put off by her putting-off words. "Well, all depends what you call nice. I always think snow looks so nice and white."

There was no response to my rather lame comment and if looks could shrivel, I would have become an immediate miniature of myself. "Leave me alone!" might as well have been written all over her.

"Look," said boldly, "I want to ask you a question."

This time she actually turned her head and fixed me with a stare. Then, she said slowly and distinctly, "And what is the question?"

That was all I needed. "Do you know Jesus?"

More quickly than I had anticipated she said, "I am an atheist," as though that settled the matter.

"Praise God! Meeting an atheist is for me like a shoemaker meeting someone with a shoe that needs mending! That means there is more work in the shop!"

"O.k., preacher man. If there is a God, then I have a lot of questions to ask you. Oh, I have heard about God and prayer and church, but I don't believe in it. There are too many things going wrong in the world for a god to exist. My personal life is a wreck, and there is no one that can help me. I came all the way to Chicago to see a doctor, and he just prattled a lot of things like self-esteem and gaining confidence that did me no good. It is all useless."

"What kind of doctor was he?"

"A psychiatrist that was highly recommended by my doctor in Ontario. Terribly expensive, but I was desperate." Her well made up face was beginning to crumple. She dabbed at her eyes with a tissue.

The airplane was taxiing down the runway in preparation for departure. Then, we were airborne.

Once we had leveled off I said, "You should try my doctor."

"Who is he?"

"His name is Jesus."

We were airborne by then,

Without warning, the lady leaned her head in her hands and began weeping silently.

I quickly looked around. I hoped no one thought I was harassing the poor woman. Then, I said, "Look, why don't you tell me about it. I will talk to Jesus about it and I know He can help you."

Then Sandra blurted out her story.

All her life, she had gone to church. She had tried to be a good woman, got a good job, and moved into an apartment. For years, she had tried to give something to society, never married, and felt she had succeeded quite well.

Then, a widower had become attracted to her, and they had started seeing each other. "Our friendship grew for a while, and then, it withered. I asked Stuart what was wrong, and at first, he did not want to tell me.

"Finally, one day, he said that he could not go on with our friendship. I was devastated and pressed him for a reason.

" 'I want to marry a Christian,' he told me! When I told him I was a Christian, he was silent."

With tears streaming down her face, Sandra told me, "I don't know what is the matter with me! All my life, I have gone to church! I believed in God and tried to do the best I could! What else does it mean to be a Christian?

"I thought I was going crazy, so I started go to psychiatrists for help. I could not understand what they were telling me, and finally, I got so desperate that I decided to fly to Chicago to see this one. Now, he let me down, too."

I sensed the despair of the woman beside me. When the flight attendant offered her something to eat, she waved it away.

I began to ask her some questions, and began praying for wisdom on how to help her.

As I talked, I realized that we were already beginning to lose altitude. I paused for a moment, and closed my eyes.

"What are you doing?" Sandra asked me curiously.

"Talking to headquarters," I said briefly.

Just then, the pilot announced, "Folks, this is Captain Tanney. Due to bad weather, we will not be landing in Syracuse. That airport is closed, due to a storm. We will be landing in Rochester and ground transportation will be provided to take you to...."

I almost laughed out loud. Talk about God answering before we even ask! The extra time was just what I wanted!

We had a blessed time as I explained to her what it meant to be a Christian. "When you repent from your sins, and ask Christ into your heart, He will give you a power you never dreamed of! You will be free from self and willing to do anything God wants you to do!"

I could sense the Spirit working in her heart. She was so desperate for help.

"Ma'am, you can not do this just so you can marry your Stuart, either," I cautioned her. "It must be a total commitment from you heart without any selfish motives."

She seemed to understand. And, by the time we had finally landed in Rochester, she was praying and asking Jesus to come and save her!

"What were you doing in Chicago?" she asked as I gave her my business card.

"Holding street meetings. Preaching to the people."

She stared at me curiously. "I marvel that I met you on the plane, of all people."

"That is the way Jesus works. He brings people into our lives that we need."

"Were there any responses in Chicago?"

I smiled. "For starters, there were the two nuns that came up to me while I was playing the accordion and singing and asked me how they could have joy in their hearts like they saw I had.

"I am sure it was strange for the people to see the Catholic women kneeling beside the sidewalk, praying with me, but I didn't care. I was too happy for them."

Shaking her head, Sandra asked, "What else?"

Our plane was stopped and the passengers were already getting to their feet.

"I did have a bad reception at first in front of a bar. The owner of the bar came out and shouted at me to go away. He said he did not want anyone singing in front of his place.

"While he was shouting at me, I changed the words of my song. 'Father, bless this man! Father in heaven, come now and bless this man. Show him your love! Let him see You! Father in heaven, come and bless this man.'

"At first, he just stood rooted to the sidewalk. Then, a strange thing happened. He began to cry."

Nodding her head, Sandra said, "I know why! All of us who carry burdens can't help be touched by the love of God, no matter how hard we try."

We were now in the airport and Sandra shook my hand. "Thank you so much for helping me! I know now what it is to be a Christian! A real one!"

"Write to me," I called after her. "God bless you!"

Less than a year later, we received a letter from Sandra. "Enclosed find a picture of Stuart and I on our honeymoon. I did not even have to tell Stuart what happened after I returned from Chicago. He said he could tell it on my face.

"God led us together and we are happily married. In the Lord!"

A verse from Psalms came to my mind, "Though I ascend into the heavens, thou art there!" Truly, God had been in the heavens with us on that airplane. And even though I had at first received a frosty reception from Sandra, God had led us to share and communicate.

"I was in prison, and ye visited me," Matthew 25:36 This verse made me see how important it was for me to go into our local jail and contact the inmates. While doing my janitorial work, I had often pitied the inmates, holed up and with nothing to do. Not only were they captured and put into prison, they were also rather captive to listen to what I told them about Jesus. Rather interestingly, it had been through my cleaning business that I had made contact with the local warden and had begun my prison ministry.

Many were the times I had the opportunity to pray with the inmates, but there were always those that seemed to resent me.

"The good news is that Jesus Christ loves you! He wants you to repent and turn your life over to Him!"

I was in a hurry that morning, dressed in my Sunday suit, on the way to conduct meetings. But because I had determined to visit the jail regularly, and I had wanted to see if my workers had cleaned properly, I had stopped in and was walking down the narrow corridor between the cells.

That day, there were a group of roudy men who must have just been hauled in because of public intoxication. I ignored them, and was speaking to a man in a cell opposite from them when suddenly, I felt something warm and wet hitting my leg.

I knew instantly what was happening. One of the drunks was urinating on me!

My first reaction was to call a guard and report the incident. Then, a wave of compassion swept over me as I remembered my own past history. I remembered all the shameful and despicable things I had done before I had become saved.

The others were yelling at the culprit, but I merely stepped closer and looking straight into his eyes, I said. "I will pray for you."

I began praying, and then, before I left, I looked at him again and said, "I will pray for you."

One man in jail, Kerney, was known to be a troublemaker. He seemed to know not to get into any serious scrapes, but he was constantly incarcerated.

"Tom, if you can get through to Kerney, you will not only help a pitiful old reprobate, you will save us a lot of headaches," the warden told me one day.

I made it a special point to try to reach the old man. At first, I was rebuffed over and over again.

Finally, one day, he began to talk," We were only married for two years, my Sally and I, when my best friend stole her from me.

"It was like a light went out and the only way I could cope was to drink until I could not think anymore. That has been my life."

"How long ago was this?" I asked.

"Twenty-seven years ago." His bleary eyes were cloudy and hopeless.

I almost gasped! A deep hidden hurt, buried inside this old man for twenty-seven years was still as real and cutting as though it had just happened!

"Kerney, hatred and bitterness are terrible twins to rule your life for so long! Don't you want to be rid of them?"

"Don't know how," was his wretched reply.

Week after week, I spent with the old man. It just seemed as though he could not grasp how God could change his heart.

One time, as I sat beside him in his cell and struggled to get him to understand, I felt so hopeless myself and in my desperation, I began to pray. While I was praying, I felt tears streaming down my face.

"You are crying!" Kerney looked at me with wonder.

I nodded and continued to pray.

"You care that much for me?" I guess he had never had anyone caring for him recently.

Before I knew it, the old man had gotten on his knees, and he began to cry. He began praying himself, and there we were in that dreary cell, two men, crying our hearts out before God.

"Kerney is a different man!" The warden was incredulous. "What ever did you do?"

Shaking my head, I answered, "It was not what I did, but what Jesus did in Kerney's heart."

The miracle happened. Kerney was released, and as far as I know, he was never in prison again. He had found forgiveness for his sins and a Friend that loved him. Praise God!

"There you are! I have been looking for you all morning!" The voice I heard was slurred and I groaned to myself.

"What is it that you want, Shay?" I asked. I could not see him, for I was under the jacked up car, trying to unscrew the oil plug.

"You jerk!" he replied. "All day yesterday you kept telling me that things would go better now. You said today, I could go with you and get a job! I need money, now!"

"Just a minute. Let me finish this job and then we can talk," I strained against the wrench handle. I knew Shay was still having withdrawal problems.

If anyone was a difficult case, Shay was. At first, he had begged for help, and when we offered him a place to stay, he used us as much as he could. Always asking for money, sneaking off and getting high on drugs, dragging himself back and crying for forgiveness and mercy; it was an ongoing problem.

"I'm going to fix you for this," I heard Shay mutter and the next thing I knew, I felt a terrific pain in my head, and then everything went black.

"Keep talking to him, Mrs. Visser," I heard a voice from far away penetrate the fog of pain I was in, "We don't know how much Mr. Visser can comprehend, but I always encourage people to keep talking. Often the sound of someone's familiar voice is enough to keep them hanging on."

I wanted to say something, ask something, but my tongue was too heavy, helpless on the bottom of my mouth. My entire head felt enormous, as though a heavy weight was resting right on top of me. I moved my right hand.

"Tom!" I heard the relief in Tina's voice. "Can you hear me? If you can, wriggle your fingers!"

I had to concentrate on how to do that. Just the effort made pains shoot through my head and I moaned slightly.

"Doctor! He responded!" Tina called out.

I began trying to put together what happened. How long had

I been here? In fact, where was I?

Doctor? I must be in a hospital! Oh, yes! I had been under my car, talking to Shay.

With great effort, I mumbled, "What happened?"

Tina's voice was right beside me. For some reason, even though I tried to open my eyes, I could not see her. "The car fell on top of your head, Tom. You are in the hospital." Her voice sounded shaky, as though she had been crying.

"How long?" I asked.

"How long was the car on your head? Until I could get help to jack the car back up from off you. I don't know how long, but it seemed hours before the rescue squad arrived."

I was trying to let it all sink in, but she had misunderstood me. "No, how long have I been in here?"

"Oh, Tom, you have been unconscious for three days! I was not sure you would ever speak to me again! I have been praying and praying. All of our friends have been praying and many have come in to see you."

I could feel myself slipping away. But I had one more question. "Shay?"

"He left," Tina told me abruptly. "He ran off right after he pushed the car over on you."

Shay did it. He tried to kill me. It was Shay.... Blackness swept over me and I knew nothing more.

I groaned in pain, trying not to move my head, yet feeling as though I had to reposition myself. Tina had left for the night, and the way I felt, I was going to have another rough time.

I had been in the hospital for two weeks. My right eye had been pushed so far out of its socket that the doctor had questioned whether I could ever see again. My head had swollen almost to twice its normal size and I could always sense how horrible I must look when a visitor came that had not been in before. No one had ever held up a mirror for me to see myself, but I knew that I must look like some prize fighter that had lost majorly. I felt like a fighter that had lost majorly.

"Why Lord?" I complained. "I have been trying to do Your work and help these young people, and now, look at this! How is it possible that You let Shay push that car on my head? I know You could have kept him from doing it! We were only trying to help Shay!"

I was really feeling discouraged. I began thinking back over our work with the people staying at our house. True, there were some that were helped and became believers, but there were also many that rejected our help and ended up back on the street, as unsaved as they had been when they had come.

"This is my pay," I grumbled. "I try to help, and I get a car pushed on my head by some drug head. My eye is popped out, my head is swollen and I have to lie here in pain. What is the use!"

I moaned in my misery.

Perhaps I moaned too loudly, for the patient in the other bed turned up the volume on the television he was watching.

The music blared and then I heard the voice of the announcer saying plainly, "Welcome Greta Schieman to the show!" There was the spattering of applause and then I heard a young woman's voice.

I was curious and opening my good eye, I could see the television screen. There was the usual introductions, and I sank back against the pillow again. But something kept pulling my mind back to the words she was saying.

"...was my former life. I want to tell you what happened to me. When I repented and gave my life to Jesus, it was marvelous to see what all happened."

Now I was greatly interested! This must be a Christian program!

"In the bars, I was always trying to get the attention of the patrons, in order to get more money. I was trying to support myself and my young daughter, so I did everything I could to get money. I felt trapped, for I knew I was doing the wrong thing.

"Then one day it happened!" I could see the young woman's eyes fill with tears, but she was smiling. "I was introduced to

Jesus, right in the middle of my act in a bar!"

Dashing away her tears, she continued, "This burly man came right up to me and said, 'What are you doing, girl?'

"My act stopped right there. Everyone just stared at him. 'Do you know that Jesus loves you? Do you know that He does not like what you are doing, but that He does love you?'

"I heard him speak to the men that were watching me, but all I could think of were the words, 'Do you know Jesus loves you?'"

Now, as I lay on the hospital bed, I began to cry. Holding back my sobs, I listened eagerly to her next words.

"That preacher man prayed for me right there in the bar, and when I went home that night, I cried out to God to help me in the name of Jesus. My life was changed!"

The host of the show interrupted. "Tell us what you are doing now."

Greta faced the camera, her eyes lit up with an inner glow. "I now help other girls that want out from that lifestyle. Together with other workers, we provide a safe place for the girls that want to escape from the clutches of their pimps. My goal is to reach as many of these poor girls for Christ Jesus that I can!"

I heard no more. I had some of my own praying and repenting to do. "God, forgive me for my complaining! I am sorry for my attitude in questioning if the work you gave me is worth it.

"Thank You for letting me hear Greta's story. You know I often wondered what happened to her, and even forgot her after a while, but now, months and months later, you let me know what happened to her! Thank You, God! I will continue on with Your work, even though it may cost my life!"

I want to say, after that, that I always stayed encouraged and kept right on with my work. But there were times that I did question just how God was going to provide for us, for the expenses were many, and there were times I became weary. However, God has been very faithful to remind me that it is His work, and to provide encouragement whenever I faltered.

One day, after I had held a street meeting in a close by town, as I was getting ready to leave from the park, a woman came up to me. "Are you Brother Tom?"

I was putting my PA system away, and I answered, "Yes, ma'am." and kept on working.

"Are you Tom Visser?" she asked again.

"Yes, and what is your problem?" I asked, finally facing her.

"Oh, I am so excited," she bubbled. "I can't believe it is really you!"

My guard went up right away, for too many times, whenever someone gets so enthusiastic to see me, they want something from me that is often not spiritual. "Well, how can I help you?"

"I just came here from Ottawa, and there was this evangelist who preached to a large crowd every evening in the church. One evening, he asked a young man to share his testimony. He mentioned your name!"

"He did?" My curiosity was aroused by now.

"Yes! This young man's name was Brian and he said he was staying at your house and finally one day, he was so ornery that you took him outside and fought with him in the yard! He said you knocked him right into God's kingdom!"

"What?" I grasped her arm. "What ever are talking about?"

"It is true," she continued. "He said that a Dutch preacher, Tom Visser, knocked him into the kingdom! He said when he left that day, he could never forget how you and your wife tried to help him and how he treated you like dirt all the time.

"It made such an impression on him - that, and I guess that you punched him to the ground - that when he heard the Gospel again, he repented and gave his life to the Lord. Now, he is a student at a Bible school and he was there to share his testimony!"

"In spite of me," I said to myself, looking at my hands. "God, You spoke to Brian in spite of me. Please, God, keep these hands from ever hitting anyone again! I thank You that Brian came to be Your son, but I am ashamed that I hit him. Knocked into the kingdom! No, loved into the kingdom!"

"Hey, buddy, do you want a ride?" I stopped my station wagon beside the road. My headlights had picked up the figure, thumbing a ride.

I needed something to do. I had been thinking of Mildred, a girl that had just left our house to go back to her old crowd. Satan had been once more trying to discourage me. So, when I had seen the hitchhiker, I had immediately hit the brakes.

The middle-aged man peered at me through the open passenger window. I had turned on the overhead light, so he could see into the car. His eyes swept over me and then looked in the back where my janitorial gear was stored.

"All right," he said, and opened the car door.

Steering back into the traffic, I waited until we were heading down the road before I asked, "Where are you going?"

"To the big church in the middle of town. They are having revival meetings there this week," he told me.

"Wonderful!" I rejoiced with him.

"You know, when you stopped and I looked in the back and saw your cleaning tools, it reminded me of an incident that happened several months ago. Almost a year ago, in fact."

I was eager to hear more. "What was that?"

"Well, you see, I had been drinking, and I was thrown into jail. This janitor came our prison to check on the cleaning his boys had done. But, he was also a preacher, and he was talking to prisoners. When his back was turned, I urinated right on his leg.

"Now, I thought he would get mad and report me to the officials, but he didn't. He just turned and looked at me and said, 'I will pray for you.'

"After I got out of jail, those words, and the look in his eyes did not go away. 'I will pray for you.' I heard the words all night long as I tried to go to sleep. 'I will pray for you.' The same words came to me the first thing in the morning.

"I could not get away from those words. Well, I tell you, I started going to church, and eventually, I became a Christian. So now, that is what your cleaning tools reminded me of."

I was laughing quietly to myself. Trying to keep a straight face, I asked him, "If you would see that janitor again, would you recognize him?"

"Oh, I am sure I would! He had a round face, smiling eyes and was very jolly. Kinda like Santa Claus!" He laughed in memory.

I reached out and turned the overhead light switch on again and faced him.

My passenger looked at me squarely in the face. "It's you!" he gasped, his eyes wide.

I switched the light off again. "You are right, it's me!"

"I am so sorry what I did to you that day! It was a terrible thing to do!"

I reached over with my right hand and said, "I forgive you. You meant it for evil, but God meant it for good. He wanted to get my attention, so I would tell you that I will pray for you. He did the rest."

Laughing, he moved over towards me and threw his arms around me. "I thank God for what you said to me!"

"Whoa! Don't make me drive into the ditch. Wait until I drop you off and then I will give you a hug!"

"I never thought I would meet you," he said as he settled down. "True, it was not so much you, as the words you said. God did not let me forget your words."

When I dropped him off, he ran over to my side of the car, and I got out. "My brother, God bless you," I told him as we embraced. "Truly, it is wonderful how the Lord works."

CHAPTER THIRTEEN

TRIED BY FIRE

"**T**ake the night off," I had told my workers. "I will do the cleaning tonight." How glibly I had spoken the evening before. Now, in the wee hours of the morning, I felt as though my sandy eyelids could scarcely remain open. It had taken me longer to do all the cleaning than I had thought it would. Well, at least I now knew just what my workers did each evening.

As soon as I saw the figure standing by the side of the road, I hit the brakes. Hitch hikers were common, and I always tried to use every opportunity I could to witness to the people thumbing a ride. Plus, it would help keep me awake.

As soon as the car stopped, the passenger door was jerked open and a huge young man jumped in. "Put 'er in park," he demanded, but gave me no time to obey. He reached over and pushed the gear shift into park.

It all happened so fast, I am not even sure today how the events took place. Suddenly, I was outside the car and two more boys were there and I was being pushed across a yard.

Now, I am a big man, but against these three, I was helpless. They were all three big burly youths, and they had me inside a garage, where they began beating me. I remembered my resolve never to fight again, but once I managed to slip away and ran into a corner. My eye was rapidly swelling shut and I was gasping from a blow to the stomach.

"What do you want?" I managed to gasp. "Take my money, but please don't beat me!"

"I fixed his truck good!" Another figure came inside the garage. "No more, 'Seek the Lord!' on the one side!" I knew then that he was trying to take my Gospel messages off the sides of my truck.

The big guy who had first grabbed me came after me again. I tried to get away, but he caught me with his huge hand and began dragging me to the center of the garage.

"You can hit me all you want, but there is one thing you can't stop me from doing," I blurted out.

"What is that?" The question was a shout.

"I will pray for you! You can't stop me from praying for you!"

A few more blows and punches were thrown at me and then I was pushed out the door.

I stumbled across the dark lawn and scrambled into my truck. My keys were still dangling in the ignition and as soon as I could, I drove out of there.

"Tom! Why are you so…" Tina stopped in mid sentence and then ran to me. "Tom! Whatever happened? Your eye is puffed up like a, like a…"

"Like a balloon?" I managed to grin.

"Worse! Whatever happened to you?"

I told her my story and her first reaction was, "We must call the police! You can tell them where it happened!"

"I know a better idea. I told them I would pray for them, and that is what I want to do! Come, will you pray with me?"

We knelt beside the sofa, and even though I was so tired and hurting from my beating, we began to pray.

The next day, I was stiff and sore from the ordeal. I tried to figure out what had infuriated the gang so much and what they had really wanted. I must have been picked at random, for it didn't seem they really were after money. I never had much cash in my wallet and they hadn't even asked me for it. It all seemed so weird. Was it the Gospel message on my truck? But they couldn't have seen it in the dark when I had first stopped. It made no sense.

When I told some of the boys that were staying in our house about it, someone said, "Gang initiation, probably. There is always some test of 'bravery' that you are asked to do to prove that you are worthy of joining."

"Well, that young man must have passed, because I sure felt his muscle. At least he picked me and not some woman or puny man!"

They all laughed at my feeble effort to joke about it.

"Someone is here!" Tina sat upright in bed and shook me.

I sat up and looked out the window. Then, I looked at the

bedside clock. Three o'clock. Headlights shone right at our house from a car that was parked in our drive.

"Is it the police?" Tina asked. We were getting somewhat used to having the police pick up someone and bring him to our New Life House, as we called our home.

"No, it is not the police," I got up and went to the window. "Its...it looks like the car that was in front of the garage where I was beat up last night!"

I started for the bedroom door.

"Tom! Don't go," Tina begged. "Call the police! Let the dog out!"

"Calm down, dear. I will go see what he wants."

When I snapped on the porch light, opened the front door, and stepped out, the door of the car immediately opened.

"Sir! It's me!" I heard the voice of the big guy from the night before. "Do not be alarmed! I am by myself."

"Yes, and what can I do for you?"

"I want to talk to you. About what you said last night."
I could not think. "What did I say last night?"

"You said you would pray for me. Those words kept running around in my brain all night and all day."

I walked across the lawn to where he stood. I reached out to put my arm around him, and I had to reach up, because he was at least a head taller than I. "Come inside."

"Tina, this is the guy that beat me up last night. This is the guy we prayed for. Will you make us some coffee?"

We sat at the kitchen table. "What is your name?" I asked.

"Joe."

"Joe, tell me what is on your mind."

Shaking his head, he said, "After you left, I thought I had proved myself as a man. I am only eighteen, but as you know, I am big and strong. I wanted to prove to the other boys that I was tough as well.

"Then, when I went to bed finally, I could not sleep. I kept hearing your words, 'I will pray for you' running over and over through my mind. I tried turning the music up, but nothing could drown your words.

"Even after I had fallen asleep, I could hear you say, 'I will pray for you' in my dreams. All day yesterday, I heard the words, no matter what I was doing.

"Tonight, when I tried going to bed, I still kept hearing the words. There was no sleep for me, so finally, I decided to come and see you."

"How did you know where Tom lived?" Tina asked, setting mugs of coffee in front of us.

"I knew. I had often seen your truck go past our house and I knew where you lived. It was not you that I picked. You were just the first one dumb enough...oh, excuse me, sir, you were just the first one that stopped."

I chuckled and took a sip of the hot coffee. "Yeah, dumb enough. But I know that God always has a plan for everything, even for those moments when we think we were dumb."

Joe looked at his cup. "What made you say you would pray for me?"

"Because God has taught me some valuable lessons." Then, I shared my testimony with him. I could tell he could identify with my earlier longing to find fulfillment. When I told him about hearing the story of the Gospel, he looked straight into my eyes. I told him about the freedom and joy that had turned my life around and then he said, "I wish I could have that."

I marvelled at his open confession. The Spirit prompted me to tell him how he could have the same joy and peace and for several hours, I talked with him.

Joe prayed the sinner's prayer that night, and from what I could tell, he was genuine and sincere. Something had touched him deeply.

When he got up to leave, morning was already streaking the eastern sky. I reached up to give him a hug, and I was almost swallowed by his bear hug. Then, he pushed away from me a little and said, "I have one more question. Why didn't you fight back the other night?"

Lifting my hands, I said, "Look at these hands. There was a time when I used them to fight. Yes, even after I was a Christian. I told the Lord afterwards I would dedicate my hands to only serve Him and not to hit anyone with them again.

"They are the Lord's hands. I will not fight, but I will pray. I have found that prayer is much stronger than my own hands, that I used to think were so strong."

Joe nodded. "I could not reason why you did not fight back. I felt powerless against you, because I was trying to make you fight so I could prove to the guys that I could win. When you did not hit back, it was as though you were winning."

I hugged him again. "Joe, that was from God. If we try to use our strength to win our battles, we only prove we are weak. But, if we let God fight for us, we become strong."

Tina and I waved to him as he left. Then, I turned to Tina and said, "Honey, it was worth the black eye and sore ribs to see this happen." Praise welled up inside of me and together we raised our arms toward heaven. "Thank You, Jesus!"

I was packing away the public address system after our weekly meeting in Gore Park. The Lord had once more given us a clear evening without rain. I marveled over and over again that God had seen fit to send us evening after evening of good weather, all summer long.

Now, autumn was here, and I was not sure how much longer we would continue. I shivered in the brisk air, ready to get inside the truck where it was warm and where Tina was waiting for me.

The three men that had stood at the edge of the crowd the last hour were the typical drifters. I glanced their way and saw them huddled on the park bench, shivering.

I placed the speakers on the back of the truck and dusted my hands. There, I was finished.

Once more, I looked at the three men. They were going to have a cold night.

"...naked, and ye gave me no clothes." Clearly and distinctly, the words ran through my mind.

I looked at my jacket. It was my last one. "Don't give it away," Tina had warned me. "You have to have at least one. Remember, you have three more places where you have been asked to speak this week."

However, the verse from God was stronger than Tina's caution.

"Here is a jacket for you," I offered the guy with no shirt my jacket.

He lifted bleary eyes in my direction.

"You can wear my shirt over your thin shirt and stay warmer," I told the second one as I began taking off my shirt. And yes, the third one was barefooted. "Even my shoes, Lord?" I questioned.

"Take my shoes. They look a little big for you, but they will keep your feet warm." I slipped out of my shoes and handed them over.

Turning, I left for the truck, the cold nipping at my bare chest.

When I opened the door and slipped inside, Tina said nothing. "Here, wear my jacket over your shoulders. You'll get cold."

I smiled at her. Yes! She understood!

Just before I turned the key to start the truck, someone knocked on the window.

A well-dressed man peered in at me. "I have heard that Tom Visser gives the shirt off his back to help the poor, but this is the first time I really believed it. I saw you give your clothes away to those bums.

"Now listen! I know you go to many places to preach, and I know it is important to have clothes for your speaking engagements. My name is Christopher Thomas and I have a clothing store of the same name. Tomorrow, you come to my store and I will make up for what you gave away." Then, he went away into the night.

Tina and I looked at each other! I began to laugh and Tina, shaking her head said in an incredulous tone, "Clothes from Christopher Thomas! The best men's store in town!"

The next day, I left that store with not only one complete set of clothes, but six! "You will soon be giving these away too, I imagine, so I might as well give you plenty!" Mr. Thomas said generously.

"God, before I ask, You answer!" My heart was filled with praise as I went home to show Tina how God had blessed me.

"Good morning, Gina!" I entered the coffee shop early one morning on the way to clean an office before business hours. The open-all-night coffee shop was right on the way and I had stopped in to get something to eat.

"Good morning, Tom," the middle-aged waitress greeted me. "What will it be this morning?"

"Coffee and a sausage biscuit will be all. I will eat a regular breakfast when I get done."

Next to me, a young man in his twenties was sitting on the stool, looking at his open hand that held a small collection of coins. He slipped off the stool and headed for the door.

"Hey, young man, sit down!" I called after him.

"I don't have enough money for coffee," he said, turning to face me.

I patted the stool beside me, "Come on, take my coffee and warm up. I can have coffee when I get home."

"Oh, thank you, sir! I have been hitchhiking all night, and I am chilled through to the bone." He wrapped his reddened fingers around the mug.

I got up to leave.

"Tom, your sausage biscuit," Gina called from the grill.

I motioned with my head toward the young man and Gina grimaced, then shrugged.

On the way home after I finished the cleaning job, I saw the young man beside the road, thumbing a ride.

I stopped and he climbed in gratefully. He held up his hands in front of the car heater.

When we reached the crossroads and I let him out, I continued on my way home. I glanced in my rear view mirror, and I saw him stamping his feet, and wrapping his arms around his chest tightly to keep warm.

I could not go on. I turned the truck around and when I came back, he looked surprised to see me.

"Here is a pair of gloves and take my boots. They are warmer than your thin shoes." He sat in the car to change into my warm boots. Then, before he got out, he turned to me. "What makes you do this to me, a stranger?"

"Because of Christ that lives in me." Then I shared with him what Jesus had done for me.

As I left him, I was blessed by the presence of the Spirit. The warmth that flowed over me was more than compensation for the loss of my boots and gloves.

Tina saw me come in without my boots. "Gave them away to someone who needed them, I guess," she said as she put a plate of scrambled eggs in front of me.

"And I am warmed by the Spirit of the Lord, "I reached up and took her hand.

After I told her my story, she got up and made me fresh coffee. "There, drink that. I already had mine and I don't think there is anyone else that will come to our door just now that you can give that away." I laughed at her and she had to smile back.

I really did not have to wait long. Some unexpected money came in and I bought myself another pair of winter boots. And, at one of the places where I cleaned, the owner approached me, "Tom, I forgot to give you your birthday gift. Happy Birthday!" and he handed me a pair of warm gloves!

I did not expect to be rewarded for giving away the boots and gloves, but I was deeply blessed to see how God provided for my needs. How I praised him for caring for these "little" needs!

"Sir, I am very sorry this has happened. We will begin an investigation immediately on how this fire started," the fire chief spoke soberly to me.

My arms were around Tina and Debbie as we stood in the middle of the morning, looking at the charred walls that used to be our house.

"Where will we live?" Debbie whimpered. Anita and Jerrid were in school and someone had gone to bring them home. Well, what was left of home.

"Honey, God will provide a place," I said almost automatically. My mind was too busy with something else.

"You have never seen smoke yet," Jason had screamed at me just that morning.

I shook my head in remembrance. I should have put an end to the meeting and spent more time with him.

After I had caught Jason smoking in the upstairs bedroom and put restraints on his activities he had stormed down the stairs, yelling, "You have never seen smoke yet," and when someone had burst into my upstairs office where I was meeting with some people, yelling, "Your house is on fire," I had been very suspicious about the origin of the blaze.

I looked around the yard, crowded with sympathetic neighbors and friends. Jason was not among them.

Several days later, I went back to the burned out house. It had stood right beside the road, separated only by a small strip of grass from the traffic. I took spray paint and wrote, "Cast down, but not destroyed" on one charred wall facing east and on the west wall I wrote, "God promised beauty for ashes!"

In the midst of trying to find another home for us, I met with various reactions from the people in our town.

"Where is the God you always say loves us?"

"Where is the Jesus you preach about now?"

Even the mayor stopped me one day and said, "Tom, when are you going to tear that old house down? It looks even worse since you sprayed graffiti on both sides, coming and going. I am not at all impressed by your actions."

"Sir, I was not trying to impress you. I want everyone to know that even though bad things happen, those who put their trust in God will always be overcomers." What he did not know was that I needed to see those words as I tried to put our lives back together again.

Our faith was tried by fire. Literally, and spiritually. Yet, I could not despair, for the Spirit of the Lord came to comfort me when I became weary with the unknowns that were ahead of us. "I give this pain to You, Lord." I could do nothing else.

Later, we were able to get a better, even bigger house. As far as I know, Jason never confessed that he was guilty of starting the fire, yet I am confident that God will not let him go. He has heard too much about Jesus to remain indifferent. I pray that he could repent before he dies and meets his Maker. As for me, I know God was with us during this firey trial.

CHAPTER FOURTEEN

SPIRIT OF READINESS

"Jake, what are you going to do tonight?" I asked my helper as we cleaned our paint brushes.

"Guess drive to the nearest town to see what is happening. Nothing going on around here."

I nodded. The job of restoring and painting Dr. Jensen's old farmhouse was paying well, but it sure was lonely out here in the country.

This was our second week. We went home weekends, drove out here on Monday mornings, then stayed in one of the rooms for the next four nights.

"And you? What will you do?" Jake wanted to know.

I rinsed my paint brush under the faucet, and shook it. "I think I'll take a walk along this road and see if I can find someone to talk to." I dried my hands on an old towel.

"Figures," Jake grinned. "You can't be long anywhere without finding someone to talk with."

I chuckled. "I guess you know me by now. But actually, you should be grateful if I find someone to talk with. That way, your ears will be spared!"

Jake grimaced and held his hands teasingly over his ears. "Yeah! Go find someone to talk to! You have already converted me!"

"I do the talking, the Spirit does the converting," I reminded him.

In the one room of the farmhouse, we had set up our cots, so we had a good place to sleep. The kitchen, well to be frank, we did not use a kitchen. We ate food we brought along from home or ate packaged food.

The two story farmhouse was clad with wooden siding, and we had prepared it for painting, scraping the flaky paint off and priming it. Then, we had to move inside yet, and repair and paint all the walls. I didn't mind it, but as I mentioned, it was lonely.

"Who are you going to find out here to talk to?" Jake asked.

"All the houses in this area belong to rich city folks that only use them for vacations or weekends. You might have to walk miles before you find someone."

I nodded in agreement. "If I don't find someone, I might just sit beside the road and sing! If I play my accordion to accompany my singing, perhaps someone will hear me and come to see what is going on. If not, I will praise God by myself!"

So, I began walking down the road. The first house looked desolate, although it was nicely fixed up and the manicured lawn was cut closely and everything kept in good shape.

I walked some more and even before I came really close to the next place, or I guess I should call it an estate, I wondered what rich dude lived there! Wow! What a place.

"Someone living in such grandeur might forget that there is another life after this! Everything a man could want!" I said to myself.

Mature shade trees spread their limbs over the two story mansion. Stone walls, underplanted with shrubbery, enclosed the lawn and partially hid the first floor of the house. A red barn and well kept outbuildings were fenced in with wooden fences. A small group of horses grazed in a paddock.

As I got closer, I caught glimpses of sleek, dark automobiles parked to one side of the house. I turned in at the paved drive and walked toward the house.

I saw the neatly dressed man come from a small building that looked like an office. He approached me.

"Good evening," I greeted him, holding out my hand. "My name is Tom Visser. What is your name?" He smiled and shook my hand. "I am a security guard for Senator Thompson. How may I help you?"

"Oh," I did some quick thinking, "Could I see Mr. Thompson, please?"

"What is your position?"

I smiled, "I am an ambassador!"

The guard looked past me. "An ambassador from where?" he asked, looking at me again. "From what country?"

"I am an ambassador for Christ," I told him plainly.

He studied me for a moment. "Why do you have an accordion

with you?"

"I want to sing for the Senator. I accompany myself on the accordion."

He eyed me again, then said, "I need to check you for any weapons."

I stretched my arms out and he patted me down. Then, he got his two-way radio, and when we heard a "Yes?" he said, "Someone to see you, sir."

Turning to me, he said, "Come this way, please."

I followed him up the brick walk toward the front entrance. We went up the wide steps and when we got to the verandah, a gentleman stepped out through the open front door.

"Good evening," he greeted me pleasantly. Then, looking at my accordion, he asked, "Are you moving in?"

I laughed, "Good evening, sir. No, I am not moving in. This is my accordion!"

He laughed with me. "What can I do for you, sir?"

I extended my hand, "My name is Tom Visser, and I came to sing for you this evening."

A half-smile lurked around his mouth. "Sing?" he questioned.

"Yes, sir. I want to sing a song for you."

Motioning with his hand, he said, "Come inside, please."

I went in and the inside was even more impressive than the outside. Hardwood floors gleamed from frequent polishings, and Oriental rugs made islands of color in the entry. We entered a large living room, bright with large windows and antique furniture.

"Have a chair," Senator Thompson pushed an armchair towards me.

"If you don't mind," I said heading for a chair with no arms, "I can play better sitting on this chair. The accordion, you know."

"Oh, yes," he agreed and sat down on a sofa, crossing his legs. "What is your work?" he wanted to know.

"My first work is to be an ambassador for Christ, but in order to support that work, I do janitorial work and paint houses.

"Sir, do you know the Lord?"

Then he told me that when he was a little boy, his stepmother often spoke to him about God and took him regularly to church. Then, when he went off to school, he quit going to church.

"I became involved with my studies and then was swept into politics." His voice grew soft and his eyes looked out the window. "After I became a Senator, the only time I go to church is for some special occasion. Too busy," he said sadly.

"Sir, what would you like me to sing?" I asked. "Is there a song from your childhood that you would like to hear?"

He gave me his attention again. "My stepmother used to sing, 'Rock of Ages' all the time. Do you know that song?"

Playing softly, I began singing the song that has touched so many lives.

"Rock of Ages, cleft for me!
Let me hide myself in Thee!
Let the water and the blood,
from thy riven side which flowed,
Be of sin, the double cure!
Cleanse me from its guilt and power!"

As I began the second verse, I heard Mr. Thompson's voice join me.

"Not the labor of my hands,
Can fulfill the law's demands.."

I heard his voice falter, and I glanced at his face. Tears were beginning to fill his eyes.

Praying for him, I continued to sing.

"Could my zeal no respite know,
Could my tears forever flow
All for sin could not atone
Thou must save and thou alone."

I did not sing the third verse right away, but only played softly. Mr. Thompson buried his head in his hand.

Then, I began singing the last verse.

"Nothing in my hand I bring
Simply to thy cross I cling

Naked, come to Thee for dress
Helpless, look to Thee for grace
Foul, I to the fountain fly!
Wash me, Savior, or I die!"

I was once more vividly reminded that in spite of all the splendor around me, all the wealth and prestige, we all were naked and helpless and filthy without Christ! I was sure that even the senator was realizing that.

"Oh, how that takes me back to my youth! My stepmother and I would sing that very song together. She is gone now, and how I miss her!"

"Did she also pray with you?" I asked, feeling sure I knew the answer.

Nodding his head, he said, "Oh, yes! She prayed with me every night when I was little!"

Placing the accordion on the floor, I got up and went over to him. "Would you like me to pray with you now?"

And amid all the splendor of that house, we knelt down on the soft rug, and prayed. I prayed for the man beside me and asked that God would speak to his softened heart. I prayed that Mr. Thompson would realize the great gift of salvation through Jesus Christ. I no longer thought of him as a powerful, influential, rich man, but just another soul who needed to understand the love of Jesus, and surrender himself to the Lordship of Christ.

Then, Mr. Thompson prayed, and at first, his words came hesitantly and slowly, but then, it was as though he forgot that I was there, and he began speaking to God.

I listened with tears in my eyes as he asked God to forgive him for neglecting the important things of life, for becoming so "big" in his own eyes that he thought he did not need God anymore.

My heart leaped for joy when I heard him ask Jesus to come into his heart and "Wash me, Savior, or I die!"

We got up from our knees, and he shook my hand gratefully. Then, he wanted to visit with me some more and before I left, he had promised me some furniture for our house. "I want to be a part of the New Life House," he told me sincerely.

"Who is going to go in there with me?" I asked the armed officers in the early morning hours. It was 4:30 and we were standing in the yard in front of Mr. Jacobsen's barn.

They looked uneasily at each other. Then, the Chief Franklin answered. "We could wait and see if he comes out. He is armed and dangerous."

"I know," I said. "You told me that when you called me."

When the phone had rung and the police asked me to come to the Jacobsens' house, it had only taken me several minutes to respond.

This request was not as strange as it may sound. Because of our work at New Life House, I was often involved with local crimes. More than once, someone had been released into our custody rather than incarcerated in jail.

"Um, you are always willing to try to talk with anyone. We thought you could try to reason with Mr. Jacobsen." The chief tried to explain.

"I am willing, Franklin, " I replied, "but I need to pray before I go in to try to talk to someone who has tried to strangle his wife with an electric cord, not to mention that he was beating his son! It will take more than bravery, or anyone armed to talk with someone like that."

The situation was indeed tense. I did not know if Mr. Jacobsen was crazy, drunk, or what. Surely, he must be a violent man.

I stood still and prayed.

A feeling of calm came over me. I lifted my head and said, "All right, I will go in. Give me a flashlight, please."

I opened the wooden door of the barn and stepped inside, shining my light straight ahead. It was only a small barn, and immediately the rays of the flashlight picked up the cringing form of a man, hunkered down on the hay. The light glinted on the long barrel of his rifle.

"Don't shoot," I said clearly. "Don't waste your bullets. If you shoot me, it would be a waste of your bullets. I don't want to harm you, but talk to you." A wave of pity swept over me as I saw the man, trying to fight some enemy, while all the while, the enemy was inside of him.

Even to myself, my little talk sounded silly, but as I walked toward him, I continued to talk to him, trying to keep his mind occupied be my words. "That's not the way to hold a gun! Here, let me hold it." I reached out in the darkness and grabbed the gun away from him.

That was the first time he moved. He sprang to feet, and swore at me. I held the gun behind my back and shone the light straight into his face.

"Listen! You are safe with me. I will not hurt you, so do not fight!" I kept my body between him and the gun.

I could smell that Mr. Jacobsen had been drinking. The old enemy had once more created chaos in a family.

"Come on outside with me," I ordered and took him by the arm and we left the barn. The yard was bright with the headlights of the officer's cars and the blinking blue light almost blinded me.

Immediately, the officers were beside me, and one whipped out handcuffs.

"Whoa!" I said as I raised my hand. "Since I went in and got the man, it seems as though I should get to say what happens next." I handed the rifle to the Chief Franklin and addressed him. "Sir, what do you say?"

"What do you mean?"

"In this case, I am the arresting officer. I went in and brought him out, so I say, do not put handcuffs on him. He is my prisoner."

"Well, well, what will you do?" he stuttered.

"Take him to my house and put him in our program," I told him firmly. "I think that will do more good for this gentleman than to clap him into jail."

"This is highly unusual," he said. "I'll have to call headquarters and get permission."

"Call Superintendant McCloskey and ask him to release Mr. Jacobsen into Tom Visser's custody."

Franklin got into his cruiser and then when he came back out, he said, "You win. McCloskey said to let you have him."

All this time, Mr. Jacobsen was having difficulty realizing what was going on. He glanced at the lighted windows in the house, but did not protest when I told him he was to get in my truck.

"How is your prisoner doing?" Chief Franklin asked me several months later when I saw him in town.

"If you come to church, you will see for yourself," I told him, smiling.

"How is that?"

"You will see his wife and son sitting in the pews and you will see Larry up front, singing in the choir!"

"I don't know how you do it," the officer said, shaking his head.

"It is not I, but the power of Jesus Christ," I answered. "Plus, you know as well as I do, Franklin, not everyone turns out so well. I grieve for everyone that we take in and they leave without becoming a believer in Jesus."

"Do not despair, Tom," Franklin told me. "I just wish we would have more houses to take in people that need help like yours. You do a wonderful service for our community."

I nodded and got into my truck. Even though I knew what he said was true, my heart still hurt for the many that were not reached.

CHAPTER FIFTEEN

SET FREE!

"**A**hh! Tokie! You have come home yet to see your mother and father," my mother said as soon as I came into her room.

"Yes, Moeder, your boy has come home to see you." I knelt down beside her bed and took her wrinkled hand in mine. "How do you feel?"

"Not so well," she replied. "I am getting weaker all the time. Soon, I think I will not be able to get out of bed."

I looked around the old, familiar room. Memories of my childhood swept over me. To be back in Werkendam was a strange feeling. Everything was much tidier than when I had left, but everything seemed smaller and the houses were crowded closer together than what I had remembered. And was our house always this small?

My father was downstairs and I could hear him shuffling around. My brothers and sisters had all married and started their own families. Even though I had met them, we were as strangers to each other, for we had spent so much of our lives apart. It was only here, with my mother that I could reconnect with my boyhood.

"Tell me about your life, your family," Mama said.

"Tina and the children are well," I told her. "Anita and Jerritt are both in school, and little Debbie is now three.

"But there are always many more people in our house than just our family," I laughed. "We have many sons and daughters, some not much younger than we are!" Then I told her about our New Life Farm.

"The animals are often a good way for us to reach these people. They enjoy grooming the horses and gathering eggs."

"Why do you do this, Tokie?" Mama asked. Papa had come upstairs and joined us.

"Because I want to tell them about Jesus and how He helps people get their lives on track. Many of these people have never felt the love from parents and so we try to love them as Jesus loves us. It is our way of telling them the Gospel."

I prayed that they could understand. "You see, when I was

lost, I did not know how to find Jesus. I was constantly searching for something to satisfy my empty heart and did not know that to serve God was complete freedom."

"You were lost, all right," Papa said.

"But now I am born again," I told him again. The first night after I had arrived home, I had shared my testimony with my parents. They had not seemed to understand, especially my father.

"Then get lost again," he said shortly. "All you ever talk about is being born again. You keep at it day and night. How are you so sure that you are right about God? How do you even know whether God exists? I would have thought you saw enough during your childhood...during the war that would tell you if a god existed, he must not care very much for humanity."

My own parents did not understand! How I longed they would see that the old Tokie they had known was now different! I thought they must understand!

"Mama, shall I sing for you? Does the old organ still work?" I went downstairs and pumping the wheezy old pedals, I began to sing hymn after hymn. My mind traveled back to the many times I had played during the occupation in order to drown out the broadcasts on the radio. The time I had been taken to the officer's camp and asked to play for their Christmas party.

Now, as I played the familiar Christmas carols for Mama, I marveled again at how often people sing the words of those glorious hymns and don't know the blessed meaning of the Gospel story they are singing. Even as I had not understood them before, when I had so glibly sang the words. Now I understood!

"Oh, holy child of Bethlehem!
Descend to us we pray!
Cast out our sin and enter in
Be born in us, today!"

The message couldn't be clearer! I prayed for my parents as I sang and pumped the organ.

"Tokie, where is your father?" Mama asked me several days later.

"He went to the market, Moeder," I told her.

"Come closer."

I went over to her bedside and sat on a chair. "Yes?" "Tokie, what makes you so happy all the time? You have something that no one else that I know seems to have. The other children are doing well in their lives, some better than you, yet none of them has what you have."

My heart began to beat faster. I wetted my lips. "Mama, it is a peace that only God can give. It happens when you become born again!"

My mother looked deeply into my eyes. "I know you keep talking about it. But I don't understand how that happens. How can I get that?"

Slowly and carefully I explained to her the need to repent from our sins, to believe that Jesus is the Son of God, and to ask Him to come and live in our hearts is to be born again.

"It doesn't make sense to me, but I do believe you because I see it in your face. You are so happy!"

"Mama, have you ever felt God speaking to you? Ever?" I knew so little about my parents' faith, or lack of it.

"Tokie, I will tell you a story. I do not forget what happened to me when I was a young girl.

"It was in the winter time, and I had spent time with some of the girls from my school. We stayed out along the dikes longer than we should have and after the other girls turned off to go to their homes, I had to go home by myself. It was out in the countryside and it got dark. I became confused and did not know which way to go to get back home.

"I had heard enough about God to cry out to Him. "Help me, God! I am lost! Take me home!' I was terrified!

"Then, in front of me, just up a little in the sky, I saw a small, shining cloud. I heard a voice, 'Follow the cloud.'

"The cloud moved slowly enough that I could keep up, and then suddenly, it vanished. I looked around me and I was in front of our home! Tokie, I never told anyone else this because I was sure no one would believe me. Do you believe me? Was it God that sent the cloud?" I could hear her voice tremble with her deep emotion.

I took her hand and rubbed it tenderly. "Yes, Mama, I believe you! I know God sent that cloud when you cried out to him for help. That is the way to get born again, Mama! You cry out to Him from your heart and He hears you!" "Tokie, help me! I want to! I know I can not live very long, and I do want to have the peace you have!"

My heart was so full, I could scarcely pray as I led my mother in her prayer to God. Then, to hear her own words, asking Jesus to forgive her sins in His name, and to enter her heart was such a joy, I could not refrain from crying for joy! My own mother! She did understand! Oh, joy! Oh, glory!

It was scarcely two years afterwards that my father sent me word. "If you want to see your mother alive, you had better come. She is already in a coma and I warn you, she may not know you all. There are days that she gives no sign of recognizing anyone."

Tina and I made arrangements and flew to Holland the next day. As we took the train to Werkendam, I prayed that I would not arrive too late to see my dear mother.

"Mama! It's Tokie!" I called to her as I stared at my mother's wrinkled face. "Can you hear me?"

I thought I saw her eyelids flicker.

"Mama! Who is this?" I asked.

Her lips began to move and she said in a slurred voice, "My preacher son from America."

"Who is with me?"

Slowly, she turned her head and looked at Tina. "Your wife," she said.

I was so happy that she was still lucid.

I pointed to Papa. "Who is that?"

"I know who he is. And I know that he does not think I know about him going out to see Wilhelmina and I am not even dead, yet!"

I did not look at Papa. I wanted to know something else. "Mama, how is it in your heart? How is it with God?"

"Tokie, can I say it like the Bible says?"

"Yes, Mama."

"Let not your heart be troubled. Ye believe in God, believe also in Me. In my Father's house are many mansions. If it were not so, I would have told you." I listened in amazement as my mama spoke those words, slowly but surely. "After you were here, Tokie, I read those words in the Bible and they are my words. Also, 'I will come again and take you where I am,' or something like that.

"I know Jesus is coming for me soon, and Tokie, I will someday see you there, too."

Tina and I were both on our knees beside her bedside, crying. Our hearts were so full of joy to know that my mother was still believing in Jesus for her salvation.

It was later, after we had returned home to Canada, that my father called and told me that my mother had died. I knew that I was going to miss her, yet I did not grieve, for I also knew that mother was in heaven.

"Thank You, God, for answering my mother's prayer when she was a young girl and planting the seed of faith in her then! But thank You even more for helping her understand in her old age, that she needed Jesus! How glorious is Your name!"

"Please, sir," I said to the superintendent of the prison, "it would mean a great deal for them to see 'The Hiding Place'. I once met Corrie ten Boom and I am sure the story of her life will greatly touch all five of these men."

"But, Mr. Visser, I do not have guards to send along with you! My staff is stretched as it is!"

I shook my head. "I am not asking for guards! All five of these men have been in the New Life Program for several years. You know their behavior! You know they have not made any trouble for you since they became Christians! I will be responsible for them, I promise!"

Mr. Sanford looked at me for a long time. I continued to pray silently, "Please, God!" I wanted so much for the prisoners to see how God had blessed Corrie and Betsie while they were in prison. How He had become so real to them!

So, God ordered it that I was able one Saturday morning to escort the five men downtown to a local theater that was showing Corrie ten Boom's testimony.

"Wow! It is great to be out!"

"Yeah, I did not think I would see downtown this soon. My sentence is for another seven years."

I could sense the excitement of the inmates. "Lord, please claim them for Your own. Don't let them get heady with this freedom!"

"Come on boys, let's make a break for it!"

I swiveled my head quickly in disbelief! What were they saying?

"Just kidding, Brother Visser! Just kidding!" They laughed at my discomfiture.

"Please!" I placed my hand on my pounding heart. "Don't give me a heart attack!"

"Hey, if you should die from a heart attack, we would still return to prison. We would not want to discredit your trust in us!"

I nodded. "Forgive me for not trusting you! I know you boys have given your lives to the Lord Jesus Christ, and it is in His power that I trust you will not try to escape!"

We sat through the entire presentation that lasted more than an hour. All of us were deeply moved.

"You met that sister?" One of the men asked on the way back.

"Yes, I used to live not far from the prison where she was first taken. Later, I met her and heard her speak."

They were silent for awhile. "If Corrie and Betsy could thank God for the lice so that the guards would not come into their dormitory to disturb their Bible study, then I know I need to be thankful in all things, like the Bible says. It always was difficult for me to understand that verse."

They began discussing the different aspects of Corrie's life and how God had used even the most difficult times of her life in order to reveal Himself to her in a loving way.

"Here we are, all six of us," I told Mr. Sanford when we walked in the jail house door.

"Well, today, Tom, you have made history. No one else has ever taken five prisoners out of here for two hours without a guard. New Life program has proven that it works."

Still, I could tell that Mr. Sanford was relieved to see us all back.

"Thank you, sir! May God bless you for allowing us to do this."

CHAPTER SIXTEEN

A DADDY
FOR ORPHANS

"I'll run down and get the mops," I told my helper, Steve, who was pushing the pile of lint together. "I left them in the back of the station wagon."

I ran down the metal steps of the glove factory. The huge rooms housing the mechanical knitters were quiet for the workers had all left for the day. Steve and I came to do the janitorial work I had contracted to do with the owners.

The late winter temperatures were still dipping into the singled digits and when I went outside in my shirtsleeves, I gasped as the cold air hit me.

I opened the back door of the car and reached in for the mops. Then, I noticed a young boy on the sidewalk on the other side of the car. I had never seen anyone walk like that!

I pulled the mops out and straightened up. Closing the door, I steeped to the rear of my parked vehicle and stared at the ludicrous sight.

"You look like a horse from the Middle Ages!" I burst out laughing. "You know, one of those steeds carrying the knights in armor, lifting their legs up into the air with a hesitation, just before setting their feet down!

"Why in the world are you walking like that?"

The dark eyes that looked up at me were pools of shadows in the light of the street lamps. "The sole of my shoe is loose and if I don't walk like this, the sole bends backwards and snow gets into my shoe."

"Well, you need a rubber band to stretch around your sole until your papa can fix that shoe," I said, rummaging in my pocket. "Or at least, tie your sole up with your shoelace."

"I don't have a papa," he said simply. "Just a mama and sisters."

"What is your name, son?" I asked, noticing his worn and skimpy clothes.

"Joey."

"Listen, Joey. I have to take these mops upstairs to where we are working, then I will be right back down." I grabbed the mops and ran upstairs.

"Steve, you and the others need to finish here. I have an errand to run."

Steve shrugged his shoulders and smiled, "Your the boss."

"I know, it looks as though I can just take off whenever I want. But this time, it is not for me." I turned to leave.

"Hey, Tom! I know you would not take off if you weren't going to help someone. We know what you do for others!"

I waved at him and hurried down the stairs.

"A pair of shoes for a boy about eleven or twelve years old," I said to the shoe clerk. " A boy this size."

Joey's eyes flickered back and forth from me to the shoe clerk. "And a pair of socks," I added as I saw the bare feet come out of the old shoes.

"They fit just right!" Joey's words were all the thanks I needed. "Oh, thank you, sir!"

"You are welcome," I patted him on his back. "Where do you live?"

"Just around the corner with Mama and my sisters."

We walked back to the glove factory together. "Good by, Joey," I called as I headed once more up the stairs.

"Anything left for me to do?" I asked going in where my workers were mopping the wooden floors.

"We are almost finished," Steve laughed. "The trash needs to be taken outside, and then we are done as soon as we finish this floor."

I grabbed two large bags and hoisted them over my shoulders. Then, I went down the stairs toward the street.

"Mister! I brought my sisters!"

There was Joey with a crowd of girls around him! Well, it looked like a crowd.

"One, two, three, four, five!" I counted out loud. "You have five sisters?"

"Yep," Joey grinned, "and they all need shoes, too!"

"Joey!" the oldest girl, who was barely in her teens, pretended to scold her brother, "don't beg!"

"Well, we do need shoes!" One of the little curly-haired girls said lifting her foot. "See?"

I patted her head. "I do see! I see that all of you need shoes. Well, well, what should we do about that?"

"Buy some at the shoe store!" the little tot replied. "Like you did for Joey!"

The other girls giggled and watched to see what I would do.

"I guess I am the grampa," I laughed and turned to Steve. "I need to find some shoes for these little ones."

"Here, Tom," Steve pressed some money in my hands. "This will help."

Like the Pied Piper, I led the children straight to the shoe store. "This will empty your bank account," a niggling voice seemed to whisper in my ear. "This is going to cost you a lot of money."

Out loud, I said to the surprised clerk, "Yes, a pair of shoes for each one! Oh, and a pair of socks, too."

When the girls were all newly shod, we were ready to leave. Just then, Joey came dashing up. "Mr. Tom! My Mama wants to see you! Come, she said to bring you to see her!" Unnoticed, he must have left and run home to tell his mother what was happening. "Please!" all the children began to beg.

"Good evening, ma'am," I entered the fifth floor apartment.

"Hello!" The mother, just a young woman, greeted me with an heavy accent. "Is good man! Tank you! Da..." words failed her, but she motioned to Joey's shoes. Tears coursed down her cheeks as she looked at her daughters' feet and saw their new shoes. "How I tank you?"

"To see the happy faces of your children is thanks enough," I laughed. "I have never seen so many pairs of bright, shining, dark eyes as I have tonight! They almost glow with a light of their own!"

She shook her head and I knew she did not understand what I was saying. The oldest girls interpreted for her.

"What country are you from?" I asked.

"From Hungary," one of the girls answered, and then spoke to her mother.

I was able to piece the story together. They had immigrated to Canada and soon afterwards, the father had died. The widow worked in a laundry while the children went to school. For three years they had no lived in Ontario, and still, it was hard for the mother to communicate in English.

"I know how you feel!" I laughed, jouncing the littlest girl on my lap. "When I first came from Europe, from Holland, it was very hard for me, too!"

The children told their mother what I had said and she smiled, talking rapidly in Hungarian.

"How can she ever repay you, Mama wants to know?"

"If you would let me pray for you and the children, then I will be repaid." I placed my hands together.

Instantly, she understood! The woman called out to her family and put her arms around them.

"Lord," I prayed as we gathered together in a circle, "Jesus said, 'Let the children come unto Me'. I am here to bring these children, and their mother, to you. Please, Lord, they have no daddy. Please be their daddy as You have promised. Look after this widow and these orphans.

"I pray that they may grow up to love You, Lord! I pray for this mother. May she depend on You for her strength, for all her needs. I claim this family for You!"

We were both weeping when I left.

"I serve the same Jesus I served when I used to live here, five years ago!" I looked out over the congregation one Sunday morning. "Do you? Has Jesus become more dear to you than ever before?"

I was only about half way through the message, when I saw a young man come in, waving his hand and looking straight up at me. For only a moment I was distracted, then I put the incident away from my mind, trying to focus on my topic. I did see there were several girls with him.

"Jesus must be the central figure in your life! If He is not Lord of your life, He is not your Savior!"

"Amen!"

Once more, I noticed the dark haired youth and the girls with him. They were paying rapt attention.

After the message, I was on my way down the aisle to the entrance door when suddenly, someone grabbed me.

"Mr. Tom! We are so glad to see you! Do you remember me?" The laughing face of the young man was right in front of me. "It's Joey! And my sisters!"

Some wheels began spinning in my head. Joey? Who was this? I meet many, many people and I did not remember a Joey! Should I?

"Mr. Tom! Remember? 'Walking like a horse from the Middle Ages!'" he tried to imitate my tone and began walking down the aisle, lifting each foot high into the air.

With a rush, my memory of the incident returned. "Joey!" I cried, giving him an enormous hug. "Now, I remember! The boy that needed shoes!"

"And all the sisters that needed shoes!" His two sisters giggled.

Even though there were other people waiting to greet me, I said, "Come, let's sit down! Tell me everything! How is your mother?"

Yes, they were all doing well. Mama no longer worked long hours in the laundry, for the older children worked to help bring in food and clothes. Yes, Mama's English had improved, they laughed.

But by far the best news was that they were Christians, baptized and a part of a local church.

"Dear Lord, once more You have brought us together," I prayed before we parted. "To be able to meet Joey and his sisters brings much joy to my heart. But more than that, is to know that you answered our prayers, and that these young people are Your children. That is more than anything I could ever ask for! You alone, are worthy of our praise! You are so good to us!"

Then, we all began lifting our feet high up into the air as we walked out of the church house, laughing together.

"Daddy, Barbara says she does not know where her Daddy is," Anita told me soberly one night. "Her mama won't tell her."

"Why are you telling me this?" I asked curiously.

"Well, you see, when I told Barbara that we go to church every Sunday to worship God, she said she doesn't believe that God cares about her. She said it was easy for me to believe, because I had parents that taught me about God. But for her, how can she believe if she doesn't know where her daddy is?" My twelve year old daughter pained for her friend.

I marveled again how children's logic cuts right across the problems in their lives and they want a direct answer.

"No one cares for me," Barbara said in flat tone. 'Mommy works all day, and Daddy is gone."

Anita's friend was often at our house, and one day, I had asked her if she knew that Jesus loves her.

"How long has your Daddy been gone?"

The shrug of her shoulder indicated she did not know. "I don't even remember him. Mama says not to talk about it."

"If you would learn to pray, God could comfort you. He wants you to know that Jesus loves you and wants to be your friend."

"Tell you what," Barbara's eyes looked straight into mine. "If God allows me to see my Daddy, I will believe in Him!"

I hardly knew what to answer. I knew that deep down inside, Barbara was trying to deal with the pain all children, and even adults, feel when they do not know where a missing parent is. How could I help her understand that God even can heal such deep wounds? She was so young!

"How old are you, Barbara?"

"I'll soon be twelve."

"Tell me what you do know about your daddy."

"Mama says he is in a nursing home because he was hurt badly in an accident. She says he is like a young child and has lost his memory. Then, she tells me not to bother her with questions."

I took her hand into mine. "I will pray for you and for your daddy. I will ask God to bring him back into your life. What is his name?"

"Kirk."

"Oh, and do you know if you have a resident here by the name of Kirk Murphy?" I asked the receptionist.

"I don't think so," the receptionist said, "but I will check the register."

I had been visiting in one of the numerous nursing homes in our part of the city, when I had remembered Barbara's request. Anita had joined me in praying for her friend.

The telephone rang and the receptionist picked up the receiver, all the time running her finger down the list of names.

Then, speaking to the caller, she looked up at me and shook her head. I turned and left.

"Hi, didn't I just see you last week at the Pine Tree Rest Home?"

The middle aged woman looked at me, "Why yes, you did! And I saw you there! You must cover a lot of ground."

"My name is Tom Visser. I am a pastor and I enjoy praying with the residents who need some encouragement."

She smiled, "You are in a much needed position. Loneliness is the greatest ill our residents face.

"I'm Mrs. Mathers, the coordinator for the nursing homes in this region. Pleased to meet you, Mr. Visser."

"Then I will probably see you again! I try to cover as many of the nursing homes as I can!" Then, a thought grabbed me!

"Hey, you don't ever remember running across a Kirk Murphy, do you?" I remembered Barbara's quest.

"Why yes, I do," came her ready answer. "We are excited about what is happening to him!"

I grabbed her hand. "Why do you say that?"

"He was hurt in an accident years ago and lost his memory, but now, he remembers more and more all the time! It is amazing!"

My heart began to beat faster. Was this the same man? "How much does he remember?"

"Mr. Murphy. Someone here to see you." The nurse spoke to one of the men in the social room.

I shook hands with him. "My name is Tom Visser. How are you today?"

The eyes that looked into my face were sunken, but not dull. "I am better than I used to be," he smiled slightly. "I used not to be able to remember anything, but now, my memory is slowly coming back."

I sat in a vacant chair next to him. "Want to tell me about it?"

"Well, I guess for many years, I was not able to do much because of my head injury. I must have just lay in bed, but now, I am beginning to remember some things." Mr. Murphy began to talk.

"They tell me I was married, but I do not remember much about that. I guess my wife is dead, for no one comes to see me." I could tell Mr. Murphy was still having some mental blocks, for he spoke very hesitantly and slowly.

"They tell me I have...had, a daughter. I wish I could see her, if she is still living."

I moved forward on my chair. "Do you know...did they tell you want her name is?"

Mr. Murphy nodded his head. "Barbara." A fat tear rolled down his cheek. "I wish I could see her," he said again. "I prayed and asked God to please let me see my daughter, my Barbara."

"You believe in God? You believe in prayer?"

Again, the nod. "Yes, He is all I have left."

I was getting so excited. "Careful, Tom," I told myself.

"Well, there is someone here that I want you to meet! I will be right back." I left the room.

I knelt in front of where Barbara was sitting. "I met your Daddy! He wants to see you. Are you ready?"

She could not speak. She nodded her head and got up from her chair.

"Mr. Murphy, look here. God has answered your prayers today! This is your daughter, Barbara!" I took the young girl by the hand, and led her over to her father.

"My daughter? Barbara?" Kirk Murphy reached out and took

her hand.

"Daddy!" Barbara half-whispered, half cried as she sat down on the chair beside her father.

"I thank God for this day," Kirk said simply. "He has answered my prayers."

Barbara nodded. Then, looking up at me she said simply, "Now, I believe, too."

CHAPTER SEVENTEEN

OUTCASTS?

"What is the special prayer meeting for?" I asked Donald, the pastor.

Grabbing me by the arm, he pulled me toward the stairs. "Come, we will gather in the basement and then we will announce what is happening! Right in our little town!" His voice was indignant.

I joined the eight or so people in the basement. I did not know any of them, except the pastor, for I had just stopped in to meet Donald and see how his church was prospering.

"The most terrible thing has happened," a plump lady said dramatically, wringing her hands when we got settled on some chairs. "I never thought to see the day!"

"Get on with it," someone urged. "Tell us what happened."

Glancing sideways at the interrupter, she sighed and said in a measured voice, pausing for effect between every word, "The... gypsies...have...rented...a ...store...building...in...town!"

Then, lifting her hands she looked around at us with wide eyes.

A tall, thin man spoke up. "What Gladys is saying, these gypsies have rented a space and put out a sign, 'Palm Reading'."

"If you would have let me finish," Gladys protested.

"So, the prayer meeting is to ask God to save the gypsies?" I asked.

There was a silence. Then, Gladys answered. "Our prayer meeting is to ask God to make the gypsies move away from here! We can't have our community threatened by this evil influence! What about our children?" I looked at Donald. Why wasn't he saying something?

"I saw one of the girls," Gladys spoke up again. "She was dressed in real weird clothes, a long skirt, a white blouse and a scandalous scarf over her black hair. I'm afraid they are up to something else, too, if you know what I mean!" She put her hands together over her stomach and looked at the floor.

"We must pray that God would have his way in this situation," Donald finally spoke up. "That our town would not be corrupted and the integrity of our lives be kept intact."

I looked at him aghast. What was he, a politician? A diplomat?

"Yes, that is what I have been saying," Gladys piped up once more. "Just that!"

"Pray them right out of town," the tall man said.

"Pray them right into the kingdom," I could not remain silent. "Pray that they would be saved. Has anyone told them that Jesus loves them?"

My words seemed to fall on the floor at my feet. Donald did not look my way and several others looked as though I made them uncomfortable.

"Come, let us bow our heads and pray," Donald tried to keep the situation under control.

I got up and left the basement. I did not feel at all comfortable with the approach the group was taking.

"Please, Lord, do not let me get angry with them," I prayed as I went back out on the street. "Keep me from having a bad attitude, but reveal to them what Christians really should be doing."

I stood at the front of the store front. The big windows were covered with opaque curtains and the wooden sign hung right above the door. "Palm Readings." Then, in smaller letters, it read, "Let us tell your future."

I knocked on the dark green door.

Almost immediately the door was opened. "Come in," a young girl's voice greeted me with a smile.

I stepped inside and saw another girl on a chair by the window.

"Please sit down," the first girl indicated an armchair, covered by a paisley shawl. "My name is Romona. I will tell your future, yes?"

I sat in the chair and when Ramona knelt in front of me and said, "Put out your hand, sir, and I will read your future," I laughed.

"Praise the Lord! I am in a similar business! The difference is that I don't read the hand, I read the Bible!"

Reaching into my pocket, I pulled out my small New

Testament and opened to the heavily used page in John 3:16. "For God so loved the world, that He gave His only begotten Son, that whosoever believeth in Him, should not perish!" I read the words loudly and clearly.

"How is that for a reading? Is it not much better than a reading of the hands? This is telling the future forever! What wonderful news that we need not perish in hell, but live with God forever!

"The whosoever includes everyone! Dutch people like me and gypsies like you!"

Ramona stayed on the floor in front of me and the other girl stared at me. I turned to her. "What is your name? Lacy? Come, and let me tell you how I know the Gospel is true."

I began telling the girls of my life as a boy. I told them of my frustrations, both as an immigrant and in my personal life. Then, I told them how Jesus had come and filled me with His Spirit after I confessed my sins and asked Jesus to save me from my sins.

The girls' eyes never left my face and they seemed mesmerized by my testimony. "You can have the same peace and joy in your lives! Jesus loves everyone and everyone can be His child! Jesus loves you, too!"

At the back of the store, I saw a curtain move and out stepped an old man, dressed in shabby clothes. As he came toward us, I saw that tobacco juice had dribbled down the sides of his mouth and made rivulets over his stubbly chin. His dark eyes were almost covered by sagging eyelids, but I forgot all about his looks when he suddenly said, "No one ever told me that Jesus loves me."

I stood up and went up to him. "Sir," I said, for I realized he must have been listening to my testimony, "if God could save a wretched man like he did me, I know His love is for you, too!"

He nodded his head slowly as if he were in deep thought. Then, he looked at the girls and nodded again. "I have never heard someone tell us that their God also cares for gypsies. We are always told to go away and not bother them. We are outcasts."

"Jesus said, 'Whosoever' and that means everyone, regardless of who he is!" I was moved deeply by the old man's words.

"Sir, come! Will you and your daughters kneel with me while I pray? Is there anyone else?" I asked waving toward the back of the store. "Behind the curtain?"

The old man shook his head, "Just us three."

Once more, the Spirit moved and we knelt and prayed. At first, I prayed and afterwards, I heard one of the girls whisper a prayer. I kept on praying and then, I heard the old man's voice, praying in his own language. I knelt with them on that old store floor for a long time, pleading with God to reveal Himself to these people who felt shunned and outcast by the people in our community.

A few days later, I went back to see how they were doing, and the sign was down, but the curtains still blocked the inside. I knocked on the door with anticipation. I was so eager to see them again!

When no one answered, I knocked again. Still, no clicking sound of the latch and so I tried to open the door. It was locked.

I went to the window and knocked. All was silent. I went around to the side door and knocked on the windowless metal door. Still, no answer.

"They left!" The clerk at the small grocery store across the street said. "I think it was the day before yesterday, I saw one of those pretty girls take down the sign and throw it into the garbage can. Then, an old man and another pretty girl came out and they walked down the road, carrying their suitcases."

At first, I felt let down. Why had they left? Why had God not allowed me to have more contact with them? Did they really understand the Gospel? Did they feel the forgiveness of Jesus in their hearts? What would happen to them, now?"

"...but God giveth the increase." Ah! Yes! I was sure that Paul often wondered how the people had received the Good News after he had preached to them. "I have planted, Apolos has watered, but God giveth the increase." I was content with knowing that I had been privileged to sow the seed of the truth in these gypsies' lives.

My mind went back to the meeting I had attended in the church basement. "Even that was appointed by God!" I marveled. "If I would not have heard about the gypsies, I would never have been led by the Spirit to seek them out! I thank You, God, even for Gladys!" I laughed out loud.

"Tina, thank you for the good supper," I pushed back my chair. I was tired from my work all day and I had fed the animals on our New Life farm before the evening meal. My body asked for rest, but my spirit was not so restful.

"You are welcome," my wife said to me. Then, she looked expectantly at me.

I nodded my head. "Yes, I am going out. I talked with a few young men in town the other night and after I spoke to them about Jesus, I asked them where they live. I want to go see them tonight."

"Dad, where is it? Where do they live?" Debbie wanted to know.

I laughed, "I am not sure you could even call it living! They told me they have some tents pitched beside the river, just at the edge of the woods. I think they just camp for awhile in one place and then move on to another place."

"Druggies," Debbie decided.

"Probably," I agreed, "but Jesus loves them all the same." Then, turning to Tina, I told her, "I might be late."

"In a tent! Daddy, there's snow outside!"

"I know, honey. That is why I want to go and see how they are. I want to check up on them."

For about three miles, I followed the river through the snow with my flashlight. "I sure hope I am on the right track," I muttered. The trail of footprints reassured me, though, that someone or some people had traveled through here fairly recently.

Ahh! A fire! Ahead, I could see the flames of a campfire making a spot of color in the darkness. "Hello! Hey, Bryce! Sam! It's Brother Tom! Hello!"

There was no answer. As I came closer, I saw a tent right

behind the fire, the flickering flames illuminating the front.

"Hello! It's Brother Tom!" Again I called.

"Hey," someone called from inside the tent. The voice sounded slurred.

I warmed myself beside the fire for several seconds, then went to the tent and pushed open the flap. "Hey, Bryce? Sam?"

"Yeah, whatayawant?" One of the inert forms managed to say. Stoned. Both of them. I shook my head in dismay.

I had hoped to talk to them about the state of their souls, but now, I knew there was no conversing with them that night.

"Are you warm enough?" I wondered. It did not feel warm inside that tent, and the two boys were not covered with blankets. I shone my flashlight inside and saw a tangled heap of blankets in one corner. I spread the blankets over the prone figures the best I could and then went back outside to the fire.

Thankfully, they had at one time gathered a huge pile of branches and limbs from dead trees together, so I threw some more wood on the fire. A shower of sparks shot upward.

Thankfully, there was no wind, for the fire was not that far away from the tent. They must have erected the tent as close to their campfire as they did to try to get some heat into their tent.

I could tell they had been camping here for awhile. There was trash littering the camping space and the snow was dirty and trampled around the tent.

I sat on a log, close to the fire. I wanted to go back home to my warm house and cozy bed, but as I looked at the fire, then at the tent, I felt bound to stay. I was sure no one would come out of the tent all night to put wood on the fire, and as cold as it was, I was not sure if they would survive the night in their spaced out state.

"I want to help them, but right now, there is nothing I can do," I said out loud to myself. "I must stay the night and see they don't freeze."

Selecting several large chunks of wood, I placed them on the fire. I stood looking at the logs. That should at least keep the fire alive until the next morning. Then, I pushed open the flap and went inside the tent. I tried not to breathe too deeply, for their was a heavy, rank smell of unwashed bodies, alcohol, and drugs inside. I wanted to air out the tent, but I knew it would only let in more cold air.

Thankfully, I was warmly dressed, but as I pushed the one boy over toward his sleeping companion, I tried to get under the blankets the best I could. At least, if there were three of us huddled together, our body heat would warm our sleeping space, even if the odors were far from refreshing.

The ground was far from soft, and I could feel the cold seeping in around the edges of the blanket. But as I lay there in that bleak and lonely tent, I began to pray for Bryce and Sam. "...and all the other 'Bryces and Sams. For the Sallys and Marys, big and little, I pray, Lord. Let them somehow know that Jesus loves them."

Several times in the night, I roused enough to shift to a different position and check to see that the boys were still covered. They must have begun to rouse from their stupor somewhat, for I heard them turning and whoever was next to me, I think it was Sam, huddled as close to me as he could to try to stay warm.

The next thing I knew, I was coughing and as I awoke, I smelled smoke! I sat up in alarm, and to my dismay, I saw that the tent had caught on fire!

I jumped up and began yelling at the boys. "Get up! Sam! Bryce! The tent is on fire!"

Flames were licking up the side closest to the campfire. I could hear the flames crackle and the glow of the blazing fire was dancing in the wind, flickering towards the tent.

Somehow, I managed to get both of the boys out of the tent. Even though they were somewhat aware of what was happening, they had a hard time staying on their feet.

"Hey! Wake up!" I yelled at them. "Your tent is on fire!"

Bryce looked at me curiously as though he could not figure out how I had come to be there.

Sam just sat on a log, watching the flames roar in the wind.

There would be no help from them. I went to the tent, and even though it was anchored to the ground, I simply pulled it away from the fire and then when the fabric collapsed, I stamped on the burning area. Thankfully, it was made of fire-retardent material and was mostly smoldering and I extinguished the smoldering fire. Then, I straightened my back and surveyed my surroundings.

I could see light beginning to streak the eastern horizon. Good! At least it was morning!

"Do you have any coffee? Or tea?" I rummaged around in the backpacks. I found some needles, but nothing else. I shook my head.

"Well, boys, there is a long walk ahead of us. I am taking you back to town with me. If I leave you out here, you will freeze to death, or burn yourselves up trying to stay warm."

The three miles back to town seemed more like thirteen, as I walked in the middle of the two staggering young men, supporting them the best I could through the snow. If I let go of Sam, he would stumble and fall into the snow, where he wanted to just lie still. Then, if I let go of Bryce to pull Sam back up into an upright position, Bryce would decide to sit down in the middle of the snow, and then, I would have to hug Sam close to my side, pull Bryce back up and start our stumbling journey back to town again. Thankfully, neither of them were big or husky, or I don't know if I could have done it.

As soon as we came to town, I stopped for a breather in front of Steadman's Store, a corner grocery market. How I hoped the store would be open, so we could go inside and warm up before going on to my house. Then, sure enough, I saw someone walk around the side of the store, go to the front door and insert his key.

I moved my boys closer in anticipation of following him inside.

"Move on!" The man said, frowning as he looked us up and down.

I realized we must look pathetic, but I was too cold to care. "Please, sir!" I begged, "we have been outside all night and are nearly frozen!" I did not consider the tent to be what you would call "inside".

"I said, 'Move on'! Do you want me to call the police?"

"Please, sir," I tried to reason, "I know we look like bums, but we really just need to come in for a little and warm up! These boys are freezing! Look at them trembling!"

Then, to my surprise, Bryce spoke up. "Brother Tom, we should pray for him!"

Sam looked at me sideways and grinned. "Yes, Brother Tom, you say prayer works. Try it on him."

For a moment I considered the situation I was in. Two drugged boys, an irate store manager, and I was to pray to God to intervene?

"O.K." I decided. "Let's pray."

I felt Bryce's hand grasp mine. "Dear Lord, you see the situation we are in. We want to come in and warm up before we go on to my house. See that this man needs to understand the love of Jesus just as much as Bryce and Sam. We are all in need of understanding how much you love us and care for us. I ask that you tell me what to do next."

I continued praying for all the homeless and then began praying for the Christians that we could show true love for everyone.

I felt a hand on my shoulder. I stopped praying and looked up. It was the manager. "Come in. Warm up."

We followed him inside and he led us over to the furnace vent. The boys sat on the floor and let the warm air flow over their blue hands.

"Sir! Brother Tom!" I heard someone call my name several days afterwards when I was downtown.

I turned to see who was speaking and I saw the manager of Steadman's store come toward me with outstretched hands.

"You know, the other morning, I had no idea it was you with those boys until you prayed. I am ashamed that I was trying at first to drive

you off."

I smiled at him. "I thank God that He changed your mind, for I was extremely tired and cold that morning. God bless you for the warmth you gave us that day."

The manager looked at his shoes. "After you left, I did some serious praying myself. I rededicated my life to God and asked Him to make me compassionate and caring. Your prayer really spoke to me that morning."

I shook his hand heartily.

"What about those boys?"

I shook my head. "Only God knows. We tried to help them, but after they dried up, they left. I pray that the seed that was planted in their hearts will someday bear fruit."

"Those poor, poor boys," the manager shook his head. "But God bless you for caring for them."

I nodded. "He already has! And I know He will continue to do so!"

CHAPTER EIGHTEEN

SPEAK THE TRUTH!

A s I followed the curving paved drive toward the stone building sitting on a small knoll, I knew this would be an unusual speaking engagement.

"Reverend Tom Visser, we want you to come and speak to our graduating class in their final month," the voice on the telephone had invited me. "Will you come?"

I guess the person inviting me, Father Theodore, he had called himself, did not know that I was willing to speak anywhere and anytime that I was invited to speak. But now, I realized, this would be different. I had never spoken in a Catholic institution, nor to a totally Catholic audience, much less to men who were entering the priesthood.

The landscaped lawns were interspersed with mature oak trees, giving a dignity and a sense of a venerable institution. My car sneaked into a parking space at the edge of the expansive paved lot.

"I come in the name of Jesus Christ! I have nothing to be ashamed of!" I reminded myself as I strode toward the entry.

Inside, I was greeted by a young man dressed in a black clerical suit. He rose, shook hands with me and said, "Come this way, please, sir. The Father Superior is waiting for you."

We went down the wide hallway, and my guide knocked on an oak paneled door. A voice answered and he pushed the door open, and bowed, indicating I could enter.

I did not know how the man expected me to greet him, but I merely went forward and with a smile, stretched out my hand. "I am Tom Visser."

The Catholic priest, all dressed up in his vestments, shook my hand warmly. "Welcome!'

"Sit down," he indicated a comfortable chair, and sat down behind his desk. "I want to brief you on the program for today.

"Since we have been doing a course in comparative religions, we have invited a number of people from different religions to come and explain their doctrine and philosophy."

I was curious, so I raised my one hand slightly. "Do you not consider this dangerous for your people, for the men studying to be priests?"

Theodore, as I called him to myself, was quick to reply. "They will be exposed to many other religions and beliefs. This course is designed for them to look into these other forms of thought, and then compare them with what the Catholic church teaches. If we try to isolate them, we are ignoring the questions that will surely someday confront them," he told me honestly.

I nodded in understanding. "They must be sure in their own minds, or they will not be good priests," I said bluntly.

With another nod, Theodore continued. "We have had leaders from the Salvation Army, from the Jehovah's Witness, from the Mormons, from the Pentecostals, and from the Baptists speak to us. You are our last speaker in the series."

I could not help asking, "Mr. Theodore! (I was not about to call him Father!) And why have you chosen me? How did you even know about me?"

It didn't seem to bother him when I addressed him as Mr. Theodore. "Because word has reached us that you are something else. A...well... kind of a street preacher...or a traveling evangelist."

"I like that! Something Else Church!" I laughed at the title.

A warning bell rang, and as the priest put his hands on the desk to rise, I asked, "Sir, could we pray together before we go in?"

I knelt on the floor and asked God to bless the assembly and to direct my words for His glory. I prayed for enlightenment for all of us in the name of Jesus.

"Even though I have been introduced as Reverend Tom Visser, and it is true, I have been to the seminary, I like to be called Brother Tom," I introduced myself from the podium, looking over the group of perhaps 200 men.

They fixed their eyes politely on me and gave me their full attention.

"I want to introduce my presentation by speaking about Mary, the mother of Jesus, called the blessed among women, like the angel Gabriel said." I wanted to meet them on familiar ground.

"I want to encourage you to be obedient to all the commands that Mary, the mother of Jesus, gave to us. Surely, she had a great insight on who her son, Jesus, the Son of God is!"

I could see heads nodding and in the front row, several vested priests glanced at each other and I could see a smile creasing their faces. Perhaps they were glad to have invited me to be the last one to speak, if I was already praising Mary, whom they held up as being almost equal to Jesus Himself.

"When Jesus and Mary were invited to the wedding at Cana was the only time I know that Mary gave a direct command. She was talking to the stewards at the wedding and she said, 'Whatever He, Jesus, tells you to do, do it.'"

Then, I paused for a moment. "So, we must look to see what Jesus tells us. That is what Mary wanted.

"Mary is not living anymore, but Jesus is! While he was on the earth, he gave us a clear commandment. 'Ye must be born again!'

"Since Mary told us to listen to what Jesus says, her message was the same, 'Ye must be born again!' That is the message that Jesus gave."

Then, I told them the wonderful, simple Gospel message that Jesus came into the world to forgive our sins, cleanse us from all iniquity, and give us new hearts.

You might think that was surely a waste of time, for these seminary students knew the Gospel story. Why, they spent hours studying the Bible and discussing the points of doctrine with their instructors.

But I did not care for all that. I wanted them to know what it meant to be born again. How Jesus longs to bring everyone into His arms and put in them a new heart.

I told them about my childhood during the war, my frustrations as a young man, and then of my adventures in Canada. They laughed at my story when I told them about my episode with the farmer's wife, but sobered as I told them about my moral descent and final desperate hours on the bridge.

"So, dear young people, you can understand that when I first felt the love of Jesus Christ for the ruined Tom I had become, I was overwhelmed! I did not know such happiness existed! I was free inside!

"Sure, I still had questions, and still do today. But I do not have to know all the answers to life. I give my unknown questions to Jesus and He carries them for me! 'Come unto Me, all ye who are weary and heavy laden! I will give you rest!'

I spoke how this rest is knowing that our sins are forgiven by the blood of Jesus and our faith in His good works, not our own good works.

I felt the Spirit move in my heart, and I told them in my simple speech just what Jesus had done for me and then I shared testimonies of the people I had worked with. I told them about Amy and Brian and Larry and Greta. How Jesus had changed their lives. I also told them about the ones whom we had tried to help, yet they had turned away from the wonderful message.

I lost track of time. I think they must have, too, for no one motioned me to stop. Then, when I sensed the time was to quit, I asked the student body to stand.

"I want to pray for you," I said, lifting my arms towards them. I prayed that the Holy Spirit would come and minister to the hearts of the listeners. I prayed that this school would become a place where Jesus Christ would meet each one of these students, and the faculty, personally. "I claim this school for Jesus Christ! I ask, Lord, that you make this a full Gospel school, teaching only the truth that is in Jesus Christ!"

I did not know the proper Catholic protocol in closing the session, but I did not care. "If you want to come forward and pray with me, asking Jesus to be not only the Savior but Lord of your life, I invite you! Come, pray with me!"

I left the speaking platform and knelt at the front and continued to pray.

"God bless you, son! Praise God!" I encouraged the ones

who were desperate enough to come and pray with me.

When we were finished praying, I got to my feet. Then, I saw him! Mr. Theodore! He was one of the kneeling ones.

I went over to him and embraced him with open arms. "Oh, I praise God!" I could not keep silent!

Mr. Theodore nodded his head. I could see he was too choked up emotionally to speak. I placed my arm around his shoulders and lifted up my other arm toward heaven. My own eyes were so filled with tears, I could barely see.

"Do not call me Father," Theodore told me. "I want to be called Brother Theodore, or Brother McCormick. I want to be a brother to all of the Christians!"

It was only a year after I had spoken at the school formerly run by the Redemptionist Fathers, whatever that was supposed to mean. Now, I had met Theodore once more.

"It is no longer a Catholic school. A group of Christian people took it over and we call it Berean Bible School. We want to continue to search the Bible and to open ourselves to the Holy Spirit to teach us the truth. I am convinced the truth is only in Jesus Christ!"

Together, we praised the Lord for the miracle he had performed in that place. I felt humbled to counted worthy to have been a small part of that work. Clearly, it was God who had touched hearts and changed lives.

I looked at the disgruntled pastor. I had never met him before, but when some people I had met asked me to come to church with them, I had accompanied them. "Oh, you must speak to the people tonight," the pastor had insisted when we were introduced. "I think you will be good for our people." Then, in a low voice, he said, "Some are so set in their ways. But others, they are beginning to question our doctrines. They say we need more than making the choice to be Christians. You look like a liberal person that can give them some good ideas on life!"

I was not sure what his theology was, but I sensed I had met someone who was more interested in lofty theology than in knowing Jesus. But wait, why had he said, "You look like a liberal person?"

Then, I immediately understood!

I still dressed much like a Dutchman. My hair, now turning white, was thick and grew around my ears. Often, I wore a Dutch cap and I still wore klompen, my favorite wooden shoes. This man probably thought I was one of the counter culture people, or in other words, a hippie.

"You tell them that being filled with the Spirit is to come to church, do good to people, and," he paused, "being open to other people's interpretation of truth!"

"I will be glad to speak to them about the truth!" I told him. But I definitely did not think I needed to be told what to say! Why ask someone to speak if you tell them what to say? A person might as well speak himself!

"I want to tell you what it means to be born again," I opened my message clearly. "Jesus said, 'Ye must be born again.' If He said, 'Must' then there is no other way to heaven."

I tried to speak very plainly. The Gospel does not need a lot of fancy words and lofty ideas. Jesus spoke plainly to us and continues to speak plainly to us through His Spirit, and we must do likewise.

I ignored the painful look on the pastor's face as I shared the wonderful message of salvation. "There is only one way to God, and that is through Jesus Christ, the Son of God. There is no other way. Not through meditation, not through Buhdda, or any other eastern or western religion. Jesus is not a religion, He is the Son of God. Through Him we are saved by our faith in His shed blood! We can be His children!"

After the message, the pastor hastily dismissed the congregation. I was stopped by some of the people from the congregation after the services were dismissed. I sensed a hunger and thirst in these dear people.

"When can you speak to us again?"

"Yes, please, we want to hear more!"

I looked around for the pastor. "I need to check with your pastor," I told them. "I will be happy to return again and speak to you."

But the pastor was not to be found. "He left," one of the boys told us.

"We will find a place to meet," someone said. "Will you come?"

We held a series of meetings in the town hall, and the townspeople invited many of their friends. God moved in a wonderful way, and before I left that town, I was blessed to see the sincerity and dedication of the congregation. Later, I heard that many of the people left that congregation and attended other, Bible believing churches. How I praise God for His faithfulness to answer the cry of sincere people, even through the ministry of a converted Dutch preacher, dressed in his native clothes!

EPILOGUE

*A*t the time of this writing, Tom is living in Ontario, Canada. Even at age 74, and in spite of failing health, he still has the same desire to "be in season, out of season, speaking the truth in love" as he has been doing for years.

"I want Jesus Christ to be glorified by my testimony and not myself. It is all because of what Jesus has done for me!" Time and again, he makes sure that his audience understands that.

There is much more that Tom has experienced than what is written in this book. For instance, there was the second fire that destroyed his rented farm and killed all his animals. There was also the time when he had a partially built wall fall on him and so cruelly break his leg that the doctor told him, "You will never walk again."

"It was prayer and faith that God wanted me to walk again that made me take off my own cast and begin a regimen of exercise that restored my leg to full use again," Tom says.

There were the false accusations he faced, the time when he was summoned to court over false charges, the misunderstandings that flare up in the wake of people who speak the truth. Yet in spite of all these things, Tom continues to follow his Star, Jesus Christ.

Perhaps the most bitter and devastating experience was when Tom, wanting to visit some family members of a man who had died, was not allowed inside because the members of a secret society, a well-known lodge, were conducting their last rites. After Tom did some research and exposed the dark practices of these societies, many of Tom's former friends, and even some of his own family, turned against him.

His wife Tina lay ill during this time, and even Tom himself was admitted to the hospital. For a while, it seemed as though Tom's life paralleled Job's life. Foreclosure was imminent on his house, his wife was dying, his children were swept into the melee, and he lost most of his material possessions.

When Tina died soon after in May, 1997, Tom mourned his wife and felt broken and desolate. Yet he says, "The Lord has given, the Lord has taken. Blessed be the name of the Lord! Though He slay me, yet will I trust Him."

After the burial of his wife, Tom decided to travel to Florida in order *to leave the controversies that surrounded him. Eventually he returned to Canada, but moved to Montreal where one of his sisters lived. He attended church services there and was dismayed by the formality and spiritual condition of the members. As usual, he spoke boldly and plainly and one lady, a widow, said, "I have come to this church for 40 years, and have never heard about a new life in Christ!"*

She repented and was baptized and today, Tom and Pat are celebrating their recent marriage! They travel in their mobile home to Florida in the winter, and recently bought a house in Ontario. Together, they continue the work that God laid on Tom so many years ago. "We tell everyone we can that Jesus loves them! The truth is too wonderful to keep silent! Look what He has done in our lives! Mission impossible, made possible by God!"

ABOUT THE AUTHOR

After teaching school for 23 years, Harvey had no plan to begin writing books. But after meeting Silvia in GOD KNOWS MY SIZE, he was inspired to write her biography. That began an eight year writing spree that continues to this day. He has authored 12 books and continues to write for Christian Aid Ministries, Berlin OH. Traveling all over the world to gather materials has been an adventure in itself, but meeting the people he writes about has become a special part of his life. "I am continually amazed at how many of God's children have wonderful stories to tell. No matter what kind of culture, race or ethnic background, the common ground for the believers in Jesus Christ is the power that changes lives for His glory!"

Harvey and Karen live in Bakersville, North Carolina and have five children and four grandchildren. They are a part of a community fellowship that is a close-knit church family. They enjoy living in the mountains and are only a short distance to the Blue Ridge Parkway.

The following titles are published by Christian Aid Ministries:

God Knows My Size 1999

They Would Not Be Silent 2001

They Would Not Be Moved 2002

War in Kosovo The Real Victors (No longer in print) 2000

Elena Strengthened Through Trials 2003

Wang Ping's Sacrifice and Other Stories 2005

Where Little Ones Cry 2004

A Small Price to Pay 2006

Tsunami From a Few That Survived 2006

The Happening, The Nickel Mines School Tragedy 2007

A Greater Call 2007

Christian Light Publications Harrisonburg, VA published:

Not in Despair 2001

Visit www.harveyyoderbooks.com for ordering additional copies and more information about any of these books. Or send an email to harveyoder@ juno.com.